Solidarity!

Jerry Houseman

Economics in a Changed Universe

Economics in a Changed Universe

Joseph E. Stiglitz, Globalization, and the Death of "Free Enterprise"

Gerald L. Houseman

LEXINGTON BOOKS

A division of
ROWMAN & LITTLEFIELD PUBLISHERS, INC.
Lanham • Boulder • New York • Toronto • Plymouth, UK

LEXINGTON BOOKS

A division of Rowman & Littlefield Publishers, Inc.
A wholly owned subsidiary of The Rowman & Littlefield Publishing Group, Inc.
4501 Forbes Boulevard, Suite 200
Lanham, MD 20706

Estover Road
Plymouth PL6 7PY
United Kingdom

British Library Cataloguing in Publication Information Available

Library of Congress Cataloging-in-Publication Data

Houseman, Gerald L.
Economics in a changed universe: Joseph E. Stiglitz, globalization, and the death of "free enterprise" / Gerald L. Houseman.
p. cm.
Includes bibliographical references and index.
ISBN-13: 978-0-7391-2714-8 (cloth: alk. paper)
ISBN-10: 0-7391-2714-4 (cloth: alk. paper)
1. Free enterprise. 2. Information theory in economics. 3. Globalization. 4. Stiglitz, Joseph E. I. Title.
HB95.H68 2008
330—dc22

2008010170

Printed in the United States of America

The paper used in this publication meets the minimum requirements of American National Standard for Information Sciences—Permanence of Paper for Printed Library Materials, ANSI/NISO Z39.48–1992.

To
JULIANA

Table of Contents

Preface

This is a study of revolution. Professor Joseph E. Stiglitz and his colleagues, George Akerlof and Michael Spence, have radically altered the study of political economy so that now we are required to take a completely different approach to markets, and because of this, to public policy as well. The problem of asymmetry of information, first addressed in 1986, now intrudes upon all that we understand about how markets function and how we should perceive them in designing policies for both the developed and the poor nations of the world.

This is also a work born of frustration. The Nobel Prize in Economics was awarded to Stiglitz, Akerlof, and Spence in 2001, but the literature of social science, and most certainly the worlds of journalism and popular culture, betray virtually no understanding of their contributions. If the evolution of this economics of information had developed along the lines of something like a normal pathway, we would now be reading and hearing different kinds and levels of conversation about politics and economics. But noise and irrelevance have prevailed; the primary objective of this effort, consequently, is to assist in making the connections between this revolution and its political and economic ramifications, for these are as significant as they are underappreciated.

This study is also devoted to bringing about much-improved economic lives to the poor people and nations of the world, the "Third World," the "less-developed countries," the sites where individuals and families struggle to survive on less than a dollar a day and, very often, can find no clean drinking water. Stiglitz has worked tirelessly to find and apply answers to this overwhelming and persistent problem, an issue tightly bound up with the humanity and security of all of us. He has sought to make the economics of information effective in our dealings with these nations, but he has also addressed and acted upon a great range of considerations, debates, definitions, dilemmas, environmental challenges, and programmatic approaches and solutions aimed at enhancing the lives of those who have little or no share of the world's wealth.

Most of the factors and issues with which he is concerned fit under the rubric of "globalization." It is within this context that Stiglitz has decided to frame his mission for change. Not surprisingly, he has found that the world does not need to consider itself an arena for zero-sum games and that, in most circumstances, solutions present themselves in ways requiring us to conclude that what is good for the poor countries can also work to the advantage of the richer, industrialized, technologically-sophisticated countries as well.

The causes to which Stiglitz is devoted are humanitarian, noble, egalitarian, and worthwhile, and this substantially eases the tasks of discerning and writing about his work and his impressive accomplishments. It is with the sincere hope that the connections between the economics of information and the broader frameworks of the world can finally and decisively be made with this effort. There is an obvious need to strengthen the case, as much as possible, for the world's poor. The depth of their despair and misery cannot be well understood from a living room armchair in America nor in any developed country. The task of understanding can be eased, however, if we can develop an appreciation of the political and economic theoretical contributions and hard data applications of the economics of information provided by Stiglitz and his colleagues as we discard the now totally-discredited ideology of "free enterprise." This is a new era for politics and economics and we must operate within a new universe of understanding.

Very few books are the product of the author alone, and this is the case here. It is with sadness that I note the passing of Professor John Kenneth Galbraith of Harvard University, who blazed earlier trails in pursuit of the truths of economics, peace, and laughter. I was most fortunately able to enjoy occasional correspondence with him over a period of more than thirty years even though I never had the pleasure of meeting him. He was invariably helpful and considerate, and I even received a letter from him during his last year; he asked me how I like Spokane, my new location, because he was always chatty as well as informative. I believe and hope that he has influenced this work. I owe a special debt to three colleagues affiliated with Eastern Washington University—Professor Emeritus Keith Quincy and Professors James Headley and Daniel Sisson. In addition, there have been important contributions from Ha-Joon Chang of Cambridge University; Jeff Madrick of the New School, the editor of *Challenge*; Ardeth Maung Thawnghmung of the University of Massachusetts at Lowell; Dr. Notrida Mandica of the *Jurnal Nasional* of Jakarta, Indonesia; E. Wayne Nafziger of

Kansas State University; George Bullion, Professor Emeritus, Indiana University; Douglas Orr of Eastern Washington University; and Ardak Yesdauletova of Eurasian National University, Astana, Kazakhstan. The insightful Werner J. Krockmeyer of Post Falls, Idaho, who has special expertise on fiscal policy, deserves special thanks, and Jeff Stamler and Frank M. Rotering, both of Brattleboro, Vermont, also offered special insights and encouragement. Students invariably provide beneficial perspectives and practical help, and these include the members of my graduate seminar in International Political Economy at Washington State University as well as Mio Kawada of Yokohama, Japan, and two special contributors and helpers, Steve Horton of Minneapolis and Sky Kauweloa of Spokane. Juliana Houseman, my wife, provides inspiration but also practical help, since her math skills are much greater than mine. No one acknowledged here is responsible for any gaffes, mistakes, or shortcomings, of course, but they all have my sincere gratitude.

GERALD L. HOUSEMAN
Spokane, Washington, February 11, 2008

Introduction

Economics is a discipline and an ambience in which questions of considerable breadth and depth are continuously raised about pricing mechanisms, market reactions, the fiscal and monetary policies of governments, the roles of corporations, technological developments and their effects, threats raised by inflationary or recessionary pressures, international trade issues, the impacts of concerns about the environment and population growth, the uses of finite resources such as oil, copper, or forests, and the distribution of wealth; and though this is not an exhaustive list, it makes us think for a moment about a more tangible side of economics than often appears to be the case as we make our way through the more eclectic writing and journals many of us have come to know and too often encounter with puzzlement or downright confusion.

Economics, after all, can be highly abstract, and the human and organizational relationships it describes and defines often fail to lend themselves to tangible or "real world" forms or dimensions. This can be appreciated when, for example, the paucity of pictures and scenes used by television to describe economic events is considered. The production of currency at the Bureau of Printing and Engraving, the headquarters building of the Federal Reserve, and concerned shoppers looking at goods and prices in supermarkets probably account for an important portion of the visual accompaniments to the voice-overs trying to tell us, in a space of a few minutes, just what is happening with interest rate policy, the price of gasoline, or the reasons why imported goods are cheaper or more expensive. We are therefore left with the task of envisioning "productivity" or "incentives" or perhaps "derivatives" as best we can. This abstract side of economics, which often appears to dominate the matters studied, can promote misunderstandings and certainly controversy.

But there is another problem with economics that is at least an equal challenge. There is a strong tendency found within the public's common-sense understandings and the popular media but also, most unfortunately, within the more rarified atmospheres of academic study and research, to place judgments and issues alongside preset concerns and beliefs about values and moral imperatives. It is therefore quite possible to witness, at academic conferences or locations within the walls of a single university or foundation, some very passionate and—it must be honestly admitted—ideological and irrational arguments and table-pounding carried out by persons presumed to be careful, unbiased, and meticulous scientists.

It is within this milieu that the principal person of this study, Professor Joseph E. Stiglitz, must work, think, judge, write, learn, teach, and deliver speeches and lectures. This cannot be easy for him, for he is an iconoclast, an original thinker, and a dedicated researcher who, with his worthy colleagues, has come up with a descriptive, helpful and revolutionary model, a paradigm that is resented, ignored, and is both under- and un-appreciated. It is a model that upsets the applecart, roils the waters of the complacent, the satisfied, and the less inquisitive types and some of their institutions, and calls for us—all of us, in fact—to change our basic ways of thinking about the realities of economics.

This new model, the economics of information, requires us to forget about the myth of "free enterprise," a term found both on bumper stickers and in bumper-sticker minds. "Free enterprise," as a result of the work of Stiglitz and his fellow researchers, is dead; and this represents a crisis for the ideological economists, political scientists, sociologists and others who have used this concept and term to describe a reality upon which some of them have based their entire research agendas and certainly their careers as well.

Their major response, as we shall see, is to continue to live in the never-land of "free enterprise" and to even (and quite shamefully) employ this term in analyzing and describing real-world phenomena and events. It can be assumed that the logic and mathematics employed in the new paradigm, the economics of information, will ultimately triumph within economics or, alternatively, the discipline can choose to make itself a faith rather than a science. This is, alas, already the case with some academics and institutions; but time and, needless to say, the strictures and rules of scientific inquiry will ultimately catch up with, isolate, and discredit such mystics.

But Stiglitz has done more than simply turn economics on its head. He could never content himself with modeling or conceptual constructs; he believes in employing applications of his findings. So he has identified a major global problem—probably *the* world problem—and has searched for answers and policy solutions to it by using the economics of information. This problem of course is our perennial battle with poverty, a puzzling dilemma often defined as that of meeting and answering the needs of the twenty percent of the people of this earth who must survive on one dollar or less per day.

His work in this area has also failed to endear him to the Establishment, the "Washington Consensus," which continues to rely upon nostrums of the past—especially privatization and deregulation, often spiced with a little corruption here or there and tied up in a package labeled—you guessed it!—"free enterprise." The myth and the mythic term, corpses though they may be, are used extensively in the analyses, reports and books and web sites of the World Bank, the International Monetary Organization (IMF), the World Trade Organization (WTO), the U. S. Agency for International Development (USAID), and many of the governments of the world, most especially the United States under the guidance of the Bush Administration.

The applications of this paradigm—in other words, the implementation of knowledge—for the concerns of the poor of this planet have seen and experienced considerable success, just as the model itself has been heralded as an unqualified accomplishment.

The present effort, then, should be seen first of all as a description of a breakthrough in economic theory, but because of the talents and determination of Stiglitz and others, this breakthrough is linked with newer studies and results in such areas as international trade and finance, aid programs, health, social welfare and infrastructure concerns, patents, banking, poverty alleviation, and problem-solving related to the needs of the peoples of the "Third World," those countries in which decent roads, dental care, sanitation, working conditions, child welfare, or income levels are as difficult to find as a clean glass of water.

It is maintained in this effort that it is important and worthwhile to know the story of this professor and his contributions and to hope—and better still, work for—the realizations that can be wrought through his thinking and his dreams of a better world.

1

A Notable Nobel

On November 8, 2001, the Nobel Prize in Economics was awarded to Joseph E. Stiglitz, George Akerlof, and Michael Spence, the founders of a revolutionary way of thinking that employs the paradigm we call the economics of information. It was a hushed but auspicious occasion, fitting well with the atmosphere of Stockholm's City Hall and its beautiful banquet room, the Blue Hall. But it was also a signal triumph for the three researchers, who had worked with great care and perseverance in perfecting their model over a period of sixteen years.

These three scholars had demonstrated, with reason, logic, and mathematics, that our traditional respect for financial bargains and settlements—the market—has been overdone, and that this is simply because no two (or more) parties involved in a deal are ever equally informed about any business contract. One of the traders invariably suffers a disadvantage because of this disequilibrium.[1] Any number of us may have already embraced such an idea intuitively, perhaps, but few or no economists had considered this problem precisely nor even seriously before these three came along, and certainly no one had developed this inherent asymmetry into a scientifically-derived proof. The arrival of this new age of information economics should be clearly regarded as a break with the past, an invalidation of certain myths about markets that have characterized our understanding of bargains since the eighteenth-century theoretical contributions of Adam Smith.

The political implications of the findings of Stiglitz, Akerlof, and Spence are staggering, immense, and manifold. Their work eviscerates the notion of "free enterprise," an idea based largely upon folklore and one particular erudite but misled Scottish moral philosopher. The ardent supporters of this myth have invariably ignored the inherent disequilibrium now discovered and emphasized by information economics. With this asymmetric flaw, "free enterprise" has been exposed as merely an ideological creation, a chimera totally lacking in any explanatory power. It is neither functional nor real nor even related to the world of economics except in the hollow and misbegotten terms of a misplaced faith that obviously needs to be foreclosed upon and forsaken.

It had long been regarded as functional, as we know well, by those who promote right-wing economic agendas, and it has been held up as serving the needs of the developing countries of the world by the World Bank, the International Monetary Fund (IMF), the World Trade Organization (WTO), and USAID, the United States Agency for International Development. Aid formulas, the opening of markets, currency changes and adjustments, and agricultural and industrial development are all seen as enhanced and, indeed, even *defined* by the rules and protocols of this extolled piece of mythic folklore.

Mythology naturally evokes such phenomena as ritual, mysticism, awe, and quite often, unspoken assumptions. All of these appear far from the rational world of economics, with its charts, math, discussion-based decision-making, and allusions and fealty to scientific method. "Free enterprise," the world has been told over and over again, had to be seen as a great "finding" bequeathed to us by economic science.

But "free enterprise" is certainly not science. It has been sustained to a great extent by the decibels of its cacophonous advocates who have tended, over the decades and centuries, to equate it with high moral standards, good health, sunshine, the American and Western heritage, and perhaps even eighteen holes of a good game at the country club. (Country clubs and golf courses, as most of us know, are perennial sources of extemporaneous "lectures" about the attributes of "free enterprise" and, for that matter, capitalism in general.) Meaner types have used "free enterprise" as a stick with which to frustrate and bash movements devoted to economic equality and opportunity, such as civil rights, feminism, labor unions, cooperatives, environmentalism, and consumer protection. We can and should now insist that such people acquaint themselves with the rudiments of information economics, which have been available to them and to the world since 1986, for we and they must now accept and hopefully appreciate a radically altered universe of economics.

The noises of "free enterprise" advocates and hoaxers were quite remote from the honor and seriousness of the Stockholm occasion (held one month after the award announcement); and in accord with the singular and remarkable nature of the moment, Stiglitz's lengthy but modest acceptance speech, the best available text on information economics, was delivered in the kind of thoughtful and reflective tones well-suited for the peaceful and long-needed interment of the defunct piece of excess we have come to know as "free enterprise."[2] This great moment of honor and undoubted appreciation of his words could have provided a tremendous contrast to Stiglitz if he had even briefly managed to reflect upon an occasion in June of the same year when he was denied access to the World Bank Building in Washington, D. C., where he had previously been employed as Chief Economist:

> . . . instead of chairing the meetings of ministers and central bankers, Stiglitz was . . . exiled safely behind the blue police cordons, the same as the nuns carrying a large wooden cross, the Bolivian union leaders, the parents of AIDS victims and other 'anti-globalization' protesters. The ultimate insider was now on the outside.[3]

His three years at the World Bank had given Stiglitz a harsh lesson in how "free enterprise" dogma was still applied against the interests (and for the most part, the wishes) of the poor of the world. It proved too difficult for him to continually observe this matching of a terrible concept with even more terrible practices carried out against the neediest, most helpless, and certainly most luckless strata of the world's population.

It had been fitting, all the same, that Stiglitz, a gordian-knot cutter for the economics discipline if there ever was one, should devote himself first and foremost to globalization and development issues, since these are without question the concerns that most touch upon the needs of the world. Information economics, Stiglitz's great theoretical but also practical contribution, could certainly find no better arena in which to provide its applications than this one.

The economic implications of this contribution are profound, but the political implications and effects, which will be felt even more deeply, are the major concern of this treatise; and this is not only because this will open new gates of justice, its most important function, but also because we can expect information economics, along with several other new developments in the social sciences, to usher in an exciting era of revised thinking as well as social change.

FREE ENTERPRISE DOES NOT EXIST, BUT AMERICA STILL BELIEVES IN IT ANYWAY

"Free enterprise" has been regarded as basic to our understanding of neoclassical economics and, indeed, to the entire realm of economic thought. It is the world of bargaining and business left in an unfettered state, free as one can possibly imagine from the actions of government, monopolistic and oligopolistic corporations or cartels, and certainly free of politico-economic organizations such as business, labor, environmental, agricultural, consumer, or other interest groups. Its efficiencies have been heralded as built-in and automatic. It has been regarded not only as characteristic of the deals of organizations, individuals, or agencies directly involved in bargaining, but as a system that sets up, in an efficient and more or less automatic manner, complementary and sometimes countervailing forces that can in some ways make up for any dislocations caused on occasion by the original parties to a deal. It has been regarded as fundamental to the workings of a capitalist system.

The most casual observer of American culture and politics is aware of the devotion to "free enterprise." Some people wince at its mention, for we know it well as a staple of political rhetoric, television commercials, bumper stickers, manifestoes, corporate advertising, stockholders' meeting business lunches, and *Wall Street Journal* and *Forbes* editorials. The term easily falls from the lips of President George W. Bush; and it was an inner faith and oft-spoken catechism clause for President Ronald Reagan, whose actual knowledge of economics was as primitive and confused as it was bombastically strident. It is the chosen topic of endless ideological "studies" carried out by this or that tax-evading "educational" foundation. It is the religion of the business press. Those still failing to get the point can see it in the "chairs of free enterprise" found in a great variety of universities (especially in the South), generously funded by persons who sometimes may actually believe that their riches are the result of it (though one of the holders of this title has told me that he does not know at all what it really means.) Third World dictators and leaders currying favor with the West work the term into their harangues. Graduation speeches can be expected to bandy the term about, and radio talk show hosts, especially the stripe we have come to know as the infamous and law-breaking types, treat it as sacrosanct. But the ultimate "truth" of the concept is perhaps found in Oklahoma City, where a boring theme park, Enterprise Square, is devoted to it. Any child, most assuredly, will prefer Disneyland to this misleading and excessively square Square.

Perspectives on "free enterprise" can obviously vary considerably. Knowledgeable observers associate it, at least tangentially, with price-fixing, the Enron Corporation, environmental threats and damage, corporate farms, consumer fraud, union-busting, the back-dating of stock options, anti-trust violations, flat tax nostrums, rationalizations for layoffs and for budget cuts in social welfare programs, privatization schemes, speculation, biased and duplicitous media, stock manipulation, deregulation, downsizing, pension scams, violation and denigration of minimum wage laws, chicanery, and corruption. Many of us have become weary of what is simply a slogan deemed useful for the arsenal of those who are just plain greedy or who have divined, sometimes with assistance from On High, that "free enterprise" legitimizes keeping people in their place as a part of some holy writ of inequality. Many conversations, readings, media presentations, power point lectures and for that matter, the most cursory of examinations, will show that the term stands for hypocrisy; and those who would doubt this could look at government handouts for corporations and the rich, cost-plus and no-bid defense contracts, tax shelters and write-offs, the gassing of several thousand Indians in Bhopal, the crack-up of the Exxon Valdez (an accident related to a pipeline project we had been told would never produce such a tragedy), the long history of union-bashing, and the ever-shifting standards of enterprising practitioners on issues such as federalism (they are both for and against states' rights, depending upon the occasion and their needs), the fates sealed by such forces against small land-holders and businesses (who also ironically claim fealty to the "free enterprise" idea), or quite recently, the filibusters permitted in the U. S. Senate, which have been both supported and condemned by such interests, depending upon the issue—or party alignments—of the occasion. Europeans, by contrast, are likely to shrug at the news of the demise of "free enterprise," for they have intuitively known about this at least since the long and hard fall of Margaret Thatcher or, more than likely, since the world-wide depression of the early 1930s.

A SECOND DEATH TO REPORT: THE "INVISIBLE HAND"

The thinker most associated with "free enterprise" is Adam Smith, the "father of capitalism," whose two-volume tome, *The Wealth of Nations*, was published in 1776. His contribution is usually cited as the authority not only for this idea but for a concretely-defined "laissez-faire" approach to markets that, according to their side's advocates, people as varied as George W. Bush, Dick Cheney, Andrew Fastow, Dan Quayle, Gordon Liddy, George Will, Alan Greenspan, Ivan Boesky, and the late Milton Friedman and Ayn Rand, stands in opposition to government and supports entrepreneurship. Smith's two volumes, however, were meant to be a critique of monopolistic corporations rather than government, though it must be added that the "invisible hand" of self-interest, in its essence a mythical concept, was set out by this severe Scottish professor of moral philosophy—economics as a discipline did not exist in his day—to show that our individual wants and needs can, without any overall guidance, lead to a good result for most of us, if not all of us.

Gross misinterpretations and even misrepresentations have been attached to Smith's effort, and these have unquestionably made him a folk hero for business lobbyists and Right-thinking people, who often elevate Smith to something like a cult figure. Some of these go so far as to make the error of stating that Smith endorsed greed, a human shortcoming he emphatically denounced and detested. Ronald Reagan, Milton Friedman, Edwin Meese III, and many others have been known to wear Adam Smith neckties to show their fealty to his *Wealth of Nations*. But some of these people have not sufficiently familiarized themselves with the text. Smith is scathing on the subject of what was then the closest equivalent to multi-national corporations, the Hanseatic League's trade monopolies, and he calls for heavy assessments against the rich in the form of a steeply progressive income tax, and in the case of those rich people given to the habits of "wastrel" wealth, he was severe to the point that he would have the government take away *all* of their money.[4] This leaves little of Smith for solid conservatives to console themselves with, though some of them might answer that there is still the self-interest creed of the "invisible hand." Or so they may have thought, for Stiglitz has demolished the "hand" as well, proving that markets really do not work in this way. It had been a comforting figment of many economists' imaginations and nothing more, but now it, too, is dead, another casualty for the Chamber of Commerce lexicon.[5] This leaves only one tangible long-term contribution of Smith—the myth of "free enterprise," which he provided with some (though not enough) lasting power because he managed to clothe it with some kind of assumed moral authority.

But no economic myth can last forever. The formal mathematical proof of Smith's belief that market outcomes are efficient was carried out by two Nobelists, Kenneth Arrow and Gerard Debreu, who specified the conditions under which this was true. (Michael Spence was one of the many students who worked under the direction and inspiration of Arrow.) The competitive equilibrium claimed in this proof, however, is not efficient when information is imperfect or markets are incomplete, according to a landmark article written later by Stiglitz and Bruce Greenwald in 1986.[6] This article, along with other works by Stiglitz and his fellows, has resulted in the undoing of "free enterprise," and this shredding is so complete that it holds the broadest possible ramifications for the discipline of political economy and, most certainly, for the politics of the world and of the nation. None of the works cited in this study or in any other are as important to the central thesis of information economics as this one, and it is recommended reading for anyone wishing to delve into the subject. The mathematics employed in this key article are quite manageable, and the reasoning and logic, though set out in what could only be called a clinical format, are easy to grasp despite the authors' tendency to understate the significance of their contribution.

It can and should be seen from the foregoing that what we have in this history is not merely a debunking of Adam Smith's "free enterprise" myth; for that myth eventually took on untoward and misleading dimensions in the hands of those who sought to employ the Edinburgh don's contributions for their own purposes. This was a disservice to his original work, even though

The Wealth of Nations managed to survive for a long time—two hundred ten years, in fact, until the publication of the Stiglitz-Greenwald article.

INFORMATION ECONOMICS: EVOLUTION AND RESEARCH

The failure of bargains and bargaining to protect both (or more) negotiators in anything resembling equal terms—in other words, the "asymmetries" of markets, the term preferred and proffered by Akerlof, Spence, and Stiglitz—was therefore well-established within the world of economics long before the Stockholm fete of 2001. Decades of labor in the vineyards resulted in production of carefully-crafted articles and essays on the topic.[7] These articles are devoted mainly to case studies of this or that industry or set of circumstances, but they have all served as building blocks for the case spelled out in the Nobel speech. Stiglitz, for example, has focused parts of his work on the insurance industry and its rate-setting while devoting an entirely different effort to the comparative market knowledge of landlords and tenant share-croppers.[8] Akerlof has demonstrated the asymmetries of the used car market and the dysfunctional "crowding out" of sound financial practices in this type of business because of a lack of attention inherent in espousal of the "free enterprise" creed.[9] (This effort suggests what we might expect to see when the great sub-prime mortgage crisis of 2007 is taken up, as it inevitably will be, for examination in the future.) Spence has performed interesting work on the signals used by businesses in taking costly but observable actions in order to improve market outcomes. A good example of the latter is the provision of dividends by firms, even in the face of costly tax considerations, in order to impress shareholders.[10]

Lay observers of the economics discipline and the machinations of its Nobel Prize awards might be understandably confused by the well-deserved attention and plaudits given to the 2001 winners because any number of past winners have achieved recognition by emphasizing the virtues and alleged efficiencies of "free enterprise" and related nostrums such as privatization, deregulation, or even the mystique of the "invisible hand." There may be some explanations—and certainly some understanding—for such a zig-zag record in conferring these honors, though perhaps none that are very good.

The three Nobelists of 2001, it should be added, are hardly the only information economics specialists. A virtual school of such experts can be found from New England to California to England, and their work is taking on an increasing importance within the discipline; and though the work and findings of information economics scholars has been proceeding and progressing for several decades, the applications of such findings are only now managing to achieve what amounts to a strong potential starting position in the policy-making arena.

However impressive such gains for information economics may be within the academic realm, the important practical services provided by these scholars and experts can be found within the vast array of societies in the world, whether they are wealthy or underdeveloped, because it is in the public arena that nearly all significant economic battles are fought. The only comparable revolution in economics in modern times was in the triumph of Keynesian principles in the 1930s, which brought tremendous changes in the policies of Western governments in their wake. Our understanding of interest rate movements, fiscal policy, inflation, recessions and depressions has increased in manifold terms as a result of Keynes' work. And his influence has been so pervasive that even conservative politicians and ideologues have grudgingly had to accept the work of the Cambridge don; they have fashioned their own neo-Keynesian versions of how governments should respond to economic events. Unfortunately, these "supply side" designs are characterized by a timing that is always too little and too late (in terms of massive deficit spending), and their policies have worked out badly even in terms of their stated aspirations. The greatest work and the most obvious benefit conferred by Keynes is found in the massive blows he was able to strike against human misery. He was able to show us how to use deficit spending and government programs to work our way out of bad economic times, bringing relief to the poor, the unemployed, the middle income people, and even the bankers.

And though less attention is given to Keynes' advice for the relatively good times, he also managed to show us the path of economic enlightenment in this sphere as well with his emphasis upon appropriate and timely deficit reductions. Not everyone has appreciated his work, as might be expected, and various unavailing attempts were made to discredit his momentous contributions.

In his final years, however, he managed to offer what some might consider a living proof of sorts for those who admire a practical orientation; for he capped off his career with a very wealthy retirement, during which he demonstrated his acuity in picking stocks and other securities. He was also good at timing markets well.

The work of Stiglitz and his comrades, though to date less well-known and inordinately limited by the reactionary atmosphere in which they have had to inaugurate their contributions, has also managed to do some good in the world; but unlike Keynes, the impact of these thinkers has largely been experienced and achieved within the less-developed nations. Most unfortunately, however, there appears to be (so far) virtually no impact upon the policies or the administration of the IMF, World Bank, WTO or other key bureaucracies. (Stiglitz enjoyed a very minor share of influence during his three-year tenure at the Bank.) The complementary views and influences of others dealing with the problems of the poor nations, such as Jeffrey Sachs and a variety of antiglobalization groups, have made important contributions in this area of concern as well, and these should not be ignored. Despite fresh and new changes in thinking, however, the old formulas for Third World development policies continue to hold sway in the U. S. and the West—privatization, deregulation, belt-tightening for the world's poorest citizens in the names of fiscal orthodoxy and debt repayment, and active and manifest discouragement for the organization of the peasantry, labor unions, or social reform groups. This has freed the inhibitions of those in the poor countries who are steeped in corruption; they have prompted measures which go well beyond any of these considerations, and usually well beyond legality and humane norms we should typically seek and expect, to insure that no significant political or social changes can or will occur. Among their violations of common decency are tolerance of abhorrent working and living conditions, disregard for the need for a clean and healthy environment, and the persistent use and abuse of child labor. Now, however, we see even George W. Bush, probably in an off-moment at a Group of Eight meeting in Scotland in July, 2005, calling for sovereign debt cancellations, greater efforts and pledges in economic aid (though far short of what is needed or even requested by other G-8 members), campaigns for public health, especially against the AIDS virus, and promotion of trade. In Bush's case, the call is for "free trade," naturally, for this infers that the religion of "free enterprise" can and must be brought to bear upon these questions; he seems, so far at least, to ignore any of the real imperatives of "fair" trade.

It is here that another eminent economist, Jeffrey Sachs, should be brought into the discussion and given due credit. It should be pointed out that though Sachs and Stiglitz certainly do not always agree on solutions to the dilemmas of economic development (probably no two economists do), both of these thinkers have been instrumental in waking up the rich nations to the persistence of what many of us regard as the world's most pressing economic problem, namely the plight of the one-fifth of the earth's population living on less than one dollar a day. Stiglitz has emphasized reforms in trade, aid, and development policies,[11] and surely Sachs would join him in these goals. Sachs makes his own contribution with a formula he believes to be the answer to world poverty: each of the wealthy nations would make sure that their aid to the poor countries would equal 0.7 percent of their gross national product, which would require more than doubling the present total of contributions. (It is fair to point out, however, that Sachs is not the original source of this formula.) The United Nations has endorsed this approach in its Millenial Economic Program.[12] Nay-sayers to such a goal are found in abundance, and they are easily able to point to aid and development failures around the globe and to the problems of corruption and maladministration; but inaction, in all events, is hardly a program, and "free enterprise" solutions are of course doomed.

The political stance of the United States on the worthy goals of aid and development has been as confusing as it is disheartening. The United Nations has been proceeding for the past several years with the outlines of a plan, the afore-mentioned Millenial Declaration, to make the 0.7 percent goal a reality. The U. S. has never endorsed this, choosing to merely watch the UN proceed with its approach. Adoption of the Declaration was slated for the General Assembly in the session beginning in September, 2005. At the last moment, however, the interim-appointed (but never Senate-confirmed) U. S. Ambassador to the UN, John Bolton, suddenly announced a broad revision of the plan in which the term "Millenial Declaration" was to be dropped along with nearly all of its goals.[13] The commitment to a 0.7 percent contribution is now off the table as far as U. S. policy is concerned. The combined effects of the work of Stiglitz and Sachs in this area of concern which, it must be insisted, is the globe's most pressing economic need, have undoubtedly helped to change the dialogues and perspectives of the world. Their influence, though it cannot be precisely traced, appears to be much greater in Europe and the less-developed countries than in North America.

INFORMATION ECONOMICS IN THE PUBLIC ARENA

The last decade of the twentieth century and the first years of the twenty-first have demonstrated, in quite practical terms, the need for close attention to market asymmetries. This has not occurred to date and this is most unfortunate, and one reason for this has been a continued fealty to the "free enterprise" myth. This faith has been far too strong and is still shockingly embraced, for reasons of interest or ignorance, by too many political and economic forces. The effect of this failure and its attendant machinations on Stiglitz's contribution, as matters have worked out, is an impressive though left-handed vindication. The vast majority of the world's poor have been chained to their squalor and hopelessness by this misplaced faith.

The economic arena, particularly within the United States, has been characterized by a devil-can-pay approach in recent years and decades that has left workers, stockholders, consumers, and the general public aghast at its rife corruption and its coddling of corporate scam artists. The Securities and Exchange Commission and any number of other federal agencies, along with the attorneys-general of many of the states (most notably Eliot Spitzer, now Governor of New York, and Bill Lockyer, now State Treasurer of California), have been forced to deal with the shortcomings and outright corruption of the multinational corporate world. Many well-known companies have been named in indictments, or have been fined or forced to seek settlements, or have been forced in some circumstances to watch their executives go to prison. Notable among these firms are American International Group, the largest American insurer; Merrill Lynch, the largest brokerage firm; and Citigroup and the Bank of America, the two largest banks; but there have also been important regulatory and criminal cases entangling not only Enron but also Merck, WorldCom, Health South, Reebok, Refco, Tyco Corporation, the infamous Adelphi Corporation, a host of mutual fund and hedge fund managements, and far too many others. Stockholders and consumers have been defrauded, pensioners have lost their rights and their hopes for an adequate retirement, patients have ingested dangerous medicines, environmental safeguards have been ignored, and labor activists have suffered egregious treatment on the receiving end of their bosses' disregard for both labor laws and human decency. Executive stock options have been routinely backdated in half of the business corporations of America (though it should be admitted that the headquarters of such firms is likely to be in Bermuda or the Cayman Islands, while their manufacturing facilities often have a China or Third World locale.) The activities of business leadership go well beyond any matters of market disequilibrium, of course, because crimes and duplicity are not supposed to be a part of any deal. But it is the case, all the same, that most of these excesses demonstrate some of the benefits of the work of information economics, as well as a further need for application of the findings and approaches produced by this school of thought. The folly of any faith in "free enterprise," needless to say, has become both well-documented and well-exposed.

The problems that have resulted from the seizure of corporate policymaking by a perverse and pervasive spirit of corruption go well beyond those enumerated by Stiglitz. There are any number of explanations offered for the sad state of corporate governance today, including a relatively new problem of a lack of innovative talent and technological development (which are problems of creeping severity in the U. S. economy), and of course a connection is invariably made here with the general quality of education as well as of information provided (or often not provided) by the media, but surely a portion of this abysmal general scene must include questions about our economic lives as persons, as a nation, and as an international community, so that any considerations of significance in this area must invariably take account of the contributions of information economics and of the problems and issues that have been raised by its advocates and practitioners.

The atmosphere that surrounds political economy, in the world and in the nation, is regarded by Stiglitz as one that cries out for change. And that is why, perhaps more than any reason, his work and the work of his colleagues is so basic and important; it most certainly is being embraced and extended with enthusiasm by thinkers and activists across the globe. This is at least a reasonable hope, and it is buttressed by its scientific basis and its humanitarian impacts. Stiglitz and his colleagues have given us a new universe of economics that is bound to provide broader opportunities for learning and information as well as improved prospects for those most in need of an altered economic environment.

2

The Economics of Information: A Model of Scientific Performance and Promise

> Information Economics represents a fundamental change in the prevailing paradigm within economics. Problems of information are central to understanding not only *market* economics but also *political economy*.
>
> —Joseph E. Stiglitz, Nobel Prize Lecture, December 8, 2001

DYNAMIC CHARACTERISTICS AND EFFECTS OF THE NEW MODEL

The gauntlet thrown down at policy-makers and the public by the information economists must be seen as a political as well as economic challenge. Many of the major debates of the past several decades have revolved around one key issue: the efficiency of the market economy and the appropriate relationship between this market and the government policies established around the world.[1] Stiglitz and his peers wrestled with these issues for a long period of time before they came up with their new paradigm and its refinement. The consequent undermining of the "laissez-faire" and "invisible hand" corruptions of economic thought, which at times have appeared to be solemn and unquestioning forms of market worship, has occurred only after lengthy intellectual excursions taken into the real world, both in the rich and developing nations. The earth-shaking result of these investigations is that Stiglitz and his colleagues in this school have been able to ascertain that markets are far from Pareto efficent.[2]

Stiglitz was born in 1943 and was raised in Gary, Indiana, a city where the long and hard fall of the industrial economy has been evident on a day-to-day basis for several decades. Gary, dilapidated and depressed in almost any precinct, is a place that presents one overriding question to the casual visitor: how can the air quality be so bad, probably the worst in the nation, when the steel industry has virtually died there? Driving past the city, which I have often done, calls for closed windows and a good air-conditioning system, but the odors will pervade the car anyway. (Do not take this to mean that I lack sympathy for the people, including the steelworkers, who live there. I am a proud member of the United Steelworkers of America, and I keep up my membership dues.) But Pareto efficient phenomena, needless to say, will sometimes appear irrelevant as measures in a world such as that which surrounds Gary; so it is no wonder that Stiglitz looked askance, from the very beginning of his career if not from the beginning of his life, at the rosy stories and scenarios about the economy told by the privileged and their toadies about the system. Gary is located at the stark front lines of the economy, a special Hell. I still recall a student who had migrated from there because her doctor advised her that her child would not be able to live in a city so lacking in decent air. An environmental activist, she had more than occasionally paddled her aluminum canoe on Lake Calumet, collecting salmonella-infected water samples near the steel mills (and sometimes from the outflows of the mills themselves) to provide to the Indiana Department of Natural Resources. She had to quit doing this when the bottom of her boat was corroded by the Lake's and the mills' chemicals. And this lake, for a long time at least, was capable of catching fire.

STIGLITZ'S LIFE, EXPERIENCES, AND CAREER

Stiglitz's life in Gary was not only a matter of confronting its physical environment, for it was also a city split deeply by class, economic, and racial divisions. It has been the scene of one of the very few de-annexations in the history of the United States, an unusual step for a local government; the present-day city of Merrillville, with its white majority, was at one time considered a part of the southernmost reaches of Gary. Stiglitz alludes to Gary in some of his presentations, including the Nobel Address, as a place that raised basic questions in his mind about the inequities of modern life.

He received his B. A. degree from Amherst College, where he had been a student body leader. He was a supporter and activist in the civil rights movement throughout his student days, which were capped by his Ph.D. from the Massachusetts Institute of Technology in 1967. It was at MIT that Stiglitz enjoyed the intellectual pleasure of working with two Nobelists, Paul Samuelson and Robert Solow, both of whom have written tributes to him.

Stiglitz became a full professor at Yale at the age of 27, but then he moved on to Stanford, Oxford, Princeton, and then Stanford again before becoming University Professor at Columbia. He was awarded the Clark Medal of the American Economic Association in 1979. A festschrift was put together in his honor in 2003, and its introductory chapter says his

> quarter-century of research established him as one of the giants of economics, his contributions ranging across every part of the discipline . . . At every university where he taught, he imbued generations of graduate students with his infectious enthusiasm for ideas and his belief in the capacity of economic analysts to lead to a better world, provided it brought to center stage the imperfections of the real world.[3]

The "real world" is certainly the ultimate concern of Stiglitz's works, and his unique contribution, information economics, is geared to this obvious point of reference. Like all theorists, Stiglitz must deal with phenomena such as abstractions and ideal cases as parts of his intellectual processes, but his focus invariably and consistently returns to the practical effects and results of his thought.

It should be noted that he is an excellent public speaker. This talent is not invariably present with great minds, but his enthusiasm for his subjects, and especially for the economics of information, contains a spark that one can see is not only thoughtful, but cheerful and even optimistic. For those familiar with economics and the problems of globalization and the poor countries, such an attitude might be regarded as misplaced, but his beliefs in reason, science, and the good will found in most people are enough to make us persevere for the causes of truth and justice. Stiglitz relates to audiences well, uses an array of cadences, tones, and emphases, and delivers his message with an ample dash of good humor.

In 1993 Stiglitz left academia to join the Clinton Administration's Council of Economic Advisers, and he eventually chaired the Council. In 1997, he left the government to become Senior Vice President and Chief Economist of the World Bank, which proved to be a fateful choice; he almost immediately took issue with the orthodoxies of this institution, crossing swords with fundamentalists on their failed principles and assumptions. *Globalization and Its Discontents*, one of his most important pieces of work, was written from this experience.[4] He resigned from the Bank in 2000, returning to the relative quiet of academic life. Some Bank officials, as well as much of Washington's officialdom, were more than happy to see him leave.

SOCIETY'S MOVES, IN FITS AND STARTS, TOWARDS THE CENTRALITY OF INFORMATION FOR THE ECONOMY

Deep dissatisfaction with the given and accepted parameters of economics, whether in the realm of macro-analysis or micro-modeling, affected the students and professors who were to become leaders in working out this new paradigm. These innovative information economists realized at an early point in their careers that any attempt to construct a new macroeconomics based upon the assumptions of traditional microeconomic modeling would fail. As Stiglitz puts it, "How could a theory that began with the assumption that all markets clear [providing a Pareto-efficient world] ever provide an explanation?"[5] The young economists in the days when Stiglitz, Akerlof, Spence, Bruce Greenwald, a prominent Stiglitz coauthor, and like-minded people who were in graduate schools assigned a daunting but overriding task to themselves: to develop ever more efficient economic models. (Some critics, then and now, believe that economics has been too devoted to model-building.) The 1960s and 1970s were a time when the enthusiasm for Keynes had fallen off markedly; he had answered a crisis situation but the advanced economies, at least, no longer appeared to be threatened by crises of a 1929 magnitude. There was also an important quibble, less well-understood by this author among others, about an apparent lack of microeconomic modeling that would undergird Keynesian theory.

Stiglitz says that he was impressed by the imperfections and the too-often dysfunctional condition of an economic system which appeared to him, even as a student, to lack any equality of access to relevant and important information. Equality is a value that is part and parcel of information economics. Workers facing layoffs, for example, are not likely to know just why their tragedy is occurring. They may have some vague ideas about competitive markets in which their employer is, for the moment at least, not doing well. They may have some notion about the ups and downs of consumer demand. They are unlikely to know any of the relevant data concerning their firm (and it is *their* firm, since they are concerned stakeholders) in terms of capital formation, short-term and long-term debt, cash flow, equity or bond markets, international trade, the interest rate maneuvers of the Federal Reserve, or the stock options, bonuses, and salaries provided for the executives. Most significantly, they are not able to protect themselves against economic uncertainties or disasters because (1) they do not know the procedures or the legal issues that would enable them to do this, (2) they do not know the lay of the land; that is, the relevant data are simply not available to them, (3) even if they managed to have access to information that could resolve the problems set out in (1) and (2), they would not be likely to possess the political nor the economic resources to deal with such an emergency. It should be added—and Stiglitz agrees with this point—that most of those who populate the lower rungs of the economic ladder often cannot really conceptualize alternative arrangements or institutions that would alleviate or solve such problems. Stiglitz suggests, for example, that insurance against economic disasters is an idea that has no acceptance at all,[6] nor for that matter, do Americans seem to know or understand a national health care system (though it invariably seems to win in the polls on the subject), nor the kinds of paid holiday, paid leave and paid vacation arrangements (usually a month per year at a minimum) found in Europe. They probably do not know the history of the demands for a "living wage" that would replace an employer's typical take-it-or-leave-it stance. They may not even be acquainted with the assumption that collective bargaining, legal since the 1930s, is available to them to provide a measure of security. The vast majority of American workers, after all, do not have union organizations to support their cause or interests (though again it should be pointed out that polls confirm, over and over again, that workers say they would prefer to have a union just as they would prefer to have health coverage). Lack of information is both the bane and the ongoing reality of their economic lives.

Against this backdrop it can be quite easily understood that the founding of information economics amounts to some new rays of hope for the system and for the people who participate in it. Information economics asks precise questions and therefore offers the prospect of finding solutions, full or at least partial, to some of the major problems of our lives. The contrasts with the past are quite fantastic: for more than a hundred years, the prevailing paradigm of neoclassical economics yielded little more than formal modeling which assumed not only a "rational man" as the purposeful actor, but that the information he possessed was *perfect.* We are to suppose that information equity was apparently not a problem at all, at least for those with advantages in the bargaining arena. The purpose in employing this rational character may of course have been noble, aiming to educate and inform us. Its utility, however, proved to be severely limited. (An earlier Nobel Prize winner, Herbert Simon, can take some of the credit for debunking the "rational man" model.)[7] So there can be little wonder that Stiglitz and his compatriots in information economics are regarded as iconoclasts; their focus demonstrates that the overriding paradigm was so flawed as to be not only inequitable but also impractical. To achieve this understanding, however, they were required to dispense with given assumptions that had been held to answer the very questions they have raised anew and have answered in a totally different way.

The questions raised by the information dilemma are deeply disturbing. Why was such a basic oversight tolerated? Was the discipline of economics simply enjoying or enduring a long era of self-satisfaction and complacency? Was it immune to human experience? Was it ahistorical in nature? The nineteenth and earlier centuries implied, after all is said and done, that something was amiss in market models, for they failed to address a host of social, political, and economic concerns. Was there a discomfited but insistent approach taken by the market and "free enterprise" advocates that could not tolerate germane questions or relevant objections to the ongoing conventional and established wisdom? All such queries are necessarily matters of conjecture, but we know that satisfactory answers to the concerns of people were neither offered nor available.

INFORMATION: VITAL TO ECONOMIC AND POLITICAL LIFE

> Information affects decision-making in every context.
>
> —Joseph E. Stiglitz, Nobel Prize Lecture

Stiglitz insists that asymmetries in information are an even more acute problem in governance than is the case in economic life.[8] He focuses much or most of his attention on the *political economy* of information, which he defines as the role of information in political processes, or collective decision-making. In this regard it should be noted that the research carried out by Stiglitz is part of a broad trend, a movement that is rediscovering, supporting, and positing the once-heralded and respected discipline of political economy as a useful tool of social science analysis.[9]

The research path for economics has been enhanced in recent years by changes that have been in the works for a quarter-century or so, and the term "political economy" has returned to its place in the sun as a redoubtable and honored category in the pursuit of knowledge. Political scientists and economists are now working together, though still in ways that are much too limited. The American Political Science Association has symbolized this rebirth through the establishment, occasional growth, and conference participation of an Organized Section on Political Economy for the past two or more decades, and this group has made notable contributions to the continued coalescence of these two strongly-related disciplines.[10] Innovators in both disciplines now appear to be carrying out the process of shattering orthodoxies and causing thoughtful economists, political scientists, and others to review a host of conventional ideas and preconceptions. A developing literature, for example, though still in an early experimental stage, relates economic behavior to biological and psychological factors affecting individuals. It can be seen that there is more than a mere reshuffling of paradigms taking place, and such changes could result in the adoption of genuinely relevant and even prescient economic policies in both the developed and less-developed nations.

It is no exaggeration to say that these fresh breezes of inquiry are perhaps the most invigorating, exciting, and challenging developments ever to occur in the history of social science. Their potential is truly pathbreaking, and the scholars now caught up in this scene can be truly grateful that they are living through such a fantastic intellectual epoch; and with its own unique contribution, information economics is undoubtedly a part of these trends.

Stiglitz is emphatic in arguing that there are asymmetries of information between those governing and the governed, a proposition difficult to challenge in these years of the Patriot Act, broadly-interpreted and -abused executive powers and so-called "signing statements," supine media, rigged presidential press conferences (and agency press conferences, as in the case of FEMA), foggy and confusing Federal Reserve Board pronouncements, obscure administrative law judgments, manipulations of statistics to the point of meaninglessness (inflation measures of questionable use to consumers, to cite one example), endless government "spin" of the country's information machinery, downplaying and discouraging the use of the Freedom of Information Act, and most tragically, electronic eavesdropping.

Speaking to the issue of information as vital for the political process comes naturally to Stiglitz, who has held significant positions of public trust. Serving as Chairman of the Council of Economic Advisers and then Chief Economist for the World Bank, a body of significance to the Third World, brought him face-to-face with the issues and decision-making of several important policy-making arenas.[11] These offices have caused him to live through a variety of experiences which have left their mark on him; and these were so searing that he takes to task the institutions with which he was formerly affiliated, and this is often done with considerable alacrity.[12]

We shall return again and again to the salutary political effects and influences brought with the founding of information economics; for these are certainly more important than any overall influence or change of direction manifested or implied in conventional economics. It should be borne in mind that, even with the apparent complexities and related problems of economic modeling, the essence of information economics is that this is an axiom holding that equal access to information, while assuredly a desirable goal, must invariably succumb to the real world, which is not likely to make room for such a consideration at any time in the near future. And while this must be stated, it remains the case that fairness and objectivity are all the same well worth striving for; that they are achievable; and that the possibilities for change may appear a bit more hopeful now than in the recent past.

3

The Death of "Free Enterprise" and the Power of Information Economics

THE PRESENT AND FUTURE EFFECTS OF THIS REVOLUTIONARY CHANGE

Certainly it is a great understatement when and if anyone points out that the full force and dynamism of the information economics model is still to be felt. Dramatic advances have occurred, especially in some very occasional applications of this knowledge to the problems of the less-developed nations, but there is still tremendous progress to be made, both in terms of the rethinking that is absolutely necessary for the sake of the various societies of the world in developing their formulations for this learning process and, quite obviously, for the policy arena as well.

The tasks of rethinking are underscored in an apt comment of John Maynard Keynes that Stiglitz incorporated into his Nobel address. Keynes pointed out, in his landmark year of 1936, that

> The ideas of economists and political philosophers, both when they are right and when they are wrong, are more powerful than is commonly understood. Indeed, the world is ruled by little else. Practical men, who believe themselves quite exempt from any intellectual influences, are usually the slaves of some defunct economist. Madmen in authority, who hear voices in the air, are distilling their frenzy from some academic scribbler of a few years back.[1]

This assuredly bears relevance to the national and world situations of today, where we witness a continuous stream of thoughtless endorsements of what may be ideologically satisfying but horribly inane nostrums set out in support of deregulation, privatization, flat-tax agendas, or other schemes amounting to little more than maneuvers within a mental straitjacket.

Discussions of this new paradigm, at least with those who are likely to be sympathetic about its possible consequences, often begin with an exercise that amounts to a friendly and understandable diversion. If it is pointed out that "free enterprise" has been exposed as a myth, a knowing rejoinder is often made that this was accomplished long ago when the patent hypocrisies of its advocates and well-wishers were first exposed. Most of us seem aware of government largesse expended in favor of corporations, for example, and this corporate welfare has been estimated conservatively in the recent past to be more than a billion dollars a year. It is now even more difficult to put a number on this in an age of Halliburton, Bechtel, and Blackwater no-bid and "cost-plus" contracts and government handouts to the oil companies. Tax favors for corporations and for the wealthy are also an important part of this picture. The Bush tax cuts, aimed mostly at the rich and perhaps the costliest in the history of the nation, as well as unprecedented considering that a war is in progress, are justified as engines that will boost economic activity and, in the long run and through the logic of "trickle-down" economics, are claimed to benefit all of us. As this is written we are still waiting for such happy times to arrive; the incomes of poor and middle-income families have been largely stagnant or in decline since 1973 except for one or two very brief periods of time. Apologists invariably use aggregate numbers of one kind or another to show that the economy is reaping great benefits from these tax cuts, but a breakdown of these by income level invariably yield a much more critical truth. Aggregate statistics are always a part of the basic reckoning in the "lifting all boats" rhetoric that is perennially so misleading. The Bush Administration sought tax cuts for the rich in a time of war, after all, and this obviously makes no sense, but it is an excellent commentary, all the same, on who is expected to make sacrifices for the system and who is not.

"Incentives" are needed, it is generally argued, so that corporations and the wealthy will open their purses for the causes of investment, economic growth, salutary effects on employment, whetting the appetites of the consumer, or perhaps (a new one) so that corporations and the wealthy will provide us with some better stewardship of the environment and the threat of global warming. It is therefore necessary, we are always told, to cut taxes on capital gains, dividend incomes, and inheritances, to cite three obvious and recent *fait accompli*, and if this is not done, the argument goes, the risk-takers will give up—for the very first time, apparently—on risk-taking. Without incentives of this kind, the money will be sealed in bank accounts, or perhaps in vaults or purses or mattresses, and will never see the light of day. It might, of course, be sent abroad, which would serve the rest of us right and, consequently, there will be no economic growth. Those who are well-to-do, in other words, would mostly quit trying to earn money with money. And if you believe in such arguments, you probably still believe in "free enterprise."

The tax cuts in the case at hand were decided upon well before any rationale was developed in order to gain support for them, but economic growth incentives are bound to be a justification, just as they were in the disastrous Reagan years. Stiglitz points out that George W. Bush's tax cuts for the rich were far from being the surest way to bring about economic stimulus. The job creation record of the second Bush Administration pales in comparison with that of recent presidents. Fewer than four million jobs were created during its first six years. Compare this to the job-creating champions of the Clinton Administration, who quintupled the Bush record with seventeen million jobs during its years. And even the corrupt Reagan Administration, beginning with an admittedly low and recessionary base, almost tripled this Administration's rate, with nine million new jobs despite setting a miserable overall record characterized by income transfers from the middle and lower income levels to the rich.[2] Incentives aimed at research and development in science and technology would probably do much more for economic growth than padding the pockets of the well-to-do, but there could also have been incentives for consumers, for education, or for other economic activities that would yield the desired results. The tax incentives Bush proposed and had passed, Stiglitz says, would never have been on his list of possible alternatives.[3]

Inequities in the tax system, needless to say, can be found in abundance, beginning with the flat-tax characteristics of the Social Security System which, sadly enough, would be expanded with the increase in levies for the System announced as a goal by Bush recently.[4] David Cay Johnston of the New York Times has demonstrated that the years since the beginning of the Reagan Administration have been an unmitigated disaster for the cause of justice within the tax system. His book, *Perfectly Legal: The Covert Campaign to Rig Our Tax System to Benefit the Super-Rich—and Cheat Everyone Else*, documents case after case of atrocious treatment of the poor and the middle class for the benefit of corporations and families who could well afford to pay their share.[5]

The tax system, in many or most respects, actually represents a perversion of "free enterprise" ideology; so it is more than a fair surmise that the condition of the system owes a great deal to the rhetoric of such "true believers." When the Reagan era began, for example, there was still a seventy percent top rate in the system, which has now been halved. The rhetoric amply performed its chore. It works in much the same way on incomes, the other end of the financial spectrum. Espousal of a minimum wage, for example, was recently declared a "Maoist" idea in *Fortune* magazine.[6]

The myth of "free enterprise" is also built around daring individuals who are willing to put up their cash and other assets for the sake of earning ever greater amounts of income; so why is society required to provide coaxers such as capital gains tax cuts to get them to invest?[7] The answer is not very clear; but John Kenneth Galbraith, another well-known name in economics, always liked to point out that poor and middle-income people need incentives as much as, and probably more than, the wealthy and well-connected do.[8] So how is the tale of "free enterprise" acted out when tax favors, subsidies, no-bid and "cost-plus" contracts, and other government favors are thrown into the mix? Why do we give money to giant food companies who grow crops and call themselves "farmers" for purposes of obtaining government favors? None of this adds up socially or morally, and the skeptic who is tired and bored with the "free enterprise" admonitions that have been blaring for years is likely to agree that this notion is finally dead.

DISCREDITED ON ITS OWN VAUNTED TERMS

It is still the case, all the same, that Stiglitz, Akerlof, and Spence have obviously accomplished much more than simply charting the inconsistencies and calling the bluffs of the "free enterprise" crowd. They have discredited this idea on its own vaunted terms. Their argument begins by examining the claims of "free enterprise" as the points of reference for study of the supposed characteristics and benefits of its "pure" form, rather than by dissecting an image of "free enterprise" drowning in the distortions caused by political maneuvering, government largesse, and corporate welfare and hypocrisy. The result is exactly what we should consider the debater's dream: proving, in the case of a distorted and corrupt entity, that the assertions made by proponents are factually wrong, but then pointing out that even if their facts could somehow improbably happen to be right in claiming that sufficient ethical guidance for the system does exist, the "free enterprise" model itself remains so flawed that it is utterly useless.

Though it is basic that an economics of information must be a part of any modern understanding of the economics discipline, it also becomes necessary to know that the essential faulty premise of the "free enterprise" ideologues is this: that economics is about efficiency (though we know that this is hardly a characteristic of the market that is always obtainable) and that issues of equity must be left to politics. The definition of "equity" is also, quite obviously, a matter that seems to be left hanging in the air, since one person's idea of it is often seen as injustice by another.

THE UTILITY AND EXPLANATORY POWER OF INFORMATION ECONOMICS

The utility and explanatory power of the new paradigm are its great intrinsic strengths. These are emphasized by the disconnect Stiglitz sees between the key aggregate variables of macroeconomics on one hand, such as consumption, inventories, real product wages, real consumption rates, and interest rates, and on the other, the assumptions of standard neoclassical economic theory. The Nobel Prize speech tells us that "if the perfect model assumptions were even approximately satisfied, the distress caused by cyclical movements in the economy would be much less than seems to be the case."[9] Much of the difficulty with the standard theory is with its inability to reach into the darker recesses of the economy to find pervasive market efficiencies that are hard to detect. The logic that is decisive in this case is that we *do* know that the malfunctions of an economy can be bad indeed; it therefore is likely that it is malfunctioning in more subtle ways most of the time. The approach of information economics provides much greater hope that such subtleties can be discovered, appreciated, and set aright, providing security and stability for an economy that will directly affect the welfare of the general public; the "free enterprise" faith quite definitely provides no such hope. But a large research agenda, all the same, lies before us.

The problem of complexity has also been ignored by many "free enterprise" stalwarts. Their pursuit of, and fealty to, the theoretical work of Adam Smith and the digressions based upon it cause wholesale disregard of the thousands of nuances found (or sometimes, merely expected to exist) in an economy. A review of almost any clutch of articles found within the covers of a single economics journal should point the reader in the direction of this complexity. The mathematically-based possibilities, when one confronts the world of economics, are virtually limitless; and information economists, aware of this, know that there is a great deal of hard spadework needed to accomplish a broadening theoretical base as their inquiry expands.[10]

The standard neoclassical theory, which defends markets that are essentially never Pareto-efficient, has focused upon only one information issue, the problem of scarcity; but consumers and business firms every day face a vast array of information problems and issues, including returns on investment, the prices and qualities of the various goods for sale in the market, the quality and efforts of workers hired, the environmental externalities of various kinds that are inevitably a part of market transactions, and so forth. In real world terms, the critical question appears to be how markets deal with information problems; and though there is no existing detailed picture of the economy that can be precisely characterized in this way, it is obvious that further research on the frontiers of information economics is needed. We do know, quite obviously, that the fundamental reason why markets with imperfect information differ from those in which information is more or less equally accessed and shared is that actions (including choices) convey information, that market participants know and realize this, and this can be expected to affect their behavior.[11]

The admission that much work needs to be done in order to refine the new paradigm stands in sharp contrast with the standard theory and the assertions of its many all-knowing advocates and sometimes deafening defenders. For these people, institutions, to cite one of the most significant variables, matter little to markets. Not even giant corporations hold great significance for them. Markets supposedly see through them and respond accordingly. The matter of information disequilibrium, in the routine of following this common course, is fatally ignored. Fealty to the markets as the arbiter of all economic interests and issues is assuredly central to their argument, so they tend to focus upon this not only because it is a matter of faith, but also because they know that virtually all economists have some respect, even though it may be grudging among, let us assume, a tiny minority of them, for the power of market forces. This can hardly save the day for these ideologues, however, because admitting that markets exist can hardly explain the shortcomings that have been exposed since 1986 and the Nobel triumph of 2001. In the matter of distribution of wealth, the greatest of the economic issues of our time and a concern of practical and utilitarian but also deep moral consequence, the market fanatics tend to believe that this does not seem to matter much as far as the functioning of the system is concerned. Stiglitz, as one might expect, takes strong issue with this.[12] It is clear that we can achieve—and thanks to Stiglitz and his colleagues we *have* achieved—much more than the standard model allows; and it is equally obvious that information economics can guide us toward this goal.

INFORMATION ECONOMISTS INSIDE AND MOSTLY OUTSIDE GOVERNMENT

Despite the current and ongoing neglect of information economics in the government and in the media, it should be admitted that, at least in the case of Stiglitz, there has been some input of his views and efforts into political systems, though there may well be no long-term effects from any of these initiatives. He served as President Clinton's Chair of the Council of Economic Advisers and on the Council for three years and he served in the leadership of the World Bank for three years as well. But it also appears, alas, that his good sense proved to be of little lasting consequence as far as any governmental bodies or their policies are concerned; and no other prominent information economics scholar appears to have been even close to the corridors of power.

There should be some marked concern over the contrast between the work accomplished to date in information economics and the malfunctioning of the U. S. economy over a broad range of issues that this school has addressed—regulatory, trade, and governmental debt imbalances, the labored, inefficient, and often corrupt dynamics of governmental budget processes, the free rein over the publicly-owned airwaves that has been given over to media and telecommunications giants, consistent attacks upon publicly-owned assets such as forests, parks, and more recently, the public roads system, a broad-scale contempt held by elite forces for the institutions of law and the judicial process, the completely irrational mania for privatization, terrible scams built around the propaganda for intellectual property concerns, and matters *ad infinitum* and *ad nauseum.*

The issue of "free enterprise" mythology, which has still not been brought to book, could and should have already been joined and dispensed with, while the cause of science, and yes, the cause of humanity could and should have been argued, heard, and intelligently discussed. The mythic alternative, amounting to little more than the monotonous drumbeat for fairy-tale economics and the ignorant and greedy programs that have been sponsored and fostered, might well have been slowed or, much more appropriately, avoided or brought to a halt if the work of Stiglitz and like-minded scholars had been heeded and had taken effect. There was never a hope for such a scenario with the George W. Bush Administration, which actively assaults and diminishes all worthwhile institutional safeguards, any few remaining equitable tax structures, and any social nets established by the New Deal and later administrations, both Democratic and Republican, that have managed to survive. Just as tragic from Stiglitz's viewpoint, however, are the failures of the Clinton Administration in articulating economic and social needs in light of the world's new realities.

Perhaps we shall see, with a variety of necessarily antecedent developments and some measure of luck, the arrival of a sense and sensibility in Washington that can include the dynamic and certainly necessary work of information economics. Such a truly revolutionary change would—and indeed must—break the grip of the "free enterprise" mythology supported by the Washington Consensus, as it is called, that is now deployed so energetically by the true believers over the range of virtually all economic issues. Such a development would begin to put us in touch both with economic realities and with ourselves. Such a hope is not impractical; and it can still lead us towards commitment to meaningful social and economic policies. Information economics is integral to this new agenda (see the Appendices at the end of this text.)

FAILING TO APPLY INFORMATION ECONOMICS HAS LED TO CHAOS, SOCIAL INEQUALITY, AND IMMENSE PRACTICAL PROBLEMS

The work of Stiglitz and his fellow information economics theorists and researchers must be appreciated from two angles. The first of these is that they have provided a new paradigm that has revolutionized economics. The second consideration, just as important, is that they are overtly or at least impliedly calling for basic reforms within the structure of market systems. The information economics school is basically unsatisfied with the current state of affairs in the worlds of commercial, governmental, and societal relationships, and they believe that the important and overarching value of fairness can be achieved and enhanced through transparency and enlargement of access to information.

Nothing less can be acceptable to those seeking this lofty goal; and though this is a matter that calls for and demands ethical dealing, there are other significant considerations as well. The information paradigm needs to be brought to bear upon our economic lives because the complexity and interdependence of these relationships hold great potential, if managed badly, for widespread chaos, panic, and even ruin. Stiglitz underscores this point several times in his recent books as he describes the various financial crises that have threatened the world economy over the past decade and a half.

Perhaps most notable among these was the Asian currency crisis of 1997 and succeeding years, an event that posed grave dangers for all of the world's economies. We barely escaped the worst consequences which could have flowed from this catastrophe, which occurred because central banks, commercial banks, and government officials strongly preferred secrecy over candor. An awareness of information economics and its precepts was exhibited, though hardly honored, in a vast array of different quarters as this crisis evolved, but the United States and the world are hardly out of the woods today since similar severe threats to the international economy persist; and dealing with these is a topic seldom broached within any context of worthwhile discussions in Washington or other centers these days.

This particular crisis demonstrated that peasants and workers in villages and rural areas of East Asia were, as seemed natural to some, kept completely out of the information loop. In Indonesia, the biggest of the most severely affected nations, everything suddenly fell apart. Cruel inflation caused the staples of rice and cooking oil to suddenly skyrocket in price, well beyond the reach of millions of people for a period of many months, during which many of them combed piles of refuse for anything of value that they could find. The currency was debased while both imports and exports shriveled; eventually, the people took to the streets and toppled the government in 1998, but the economy was crippled for years to come.[13] One of the long-term effects of this cataclysmic period is Indonesia's stated position that an agenda of no international trade agreements of any kind, within the WTO nor with any other agency, shall be preferred over any burden of new agreements, especially in the matter of agricultural issues.[14]

The policy-makers and bureaucrats of the IMF, and certainly in the World Bank as well, apparently did not foresee the shockwaves of the Asian currency crisis, and according to Stiglitz, their misleading "market-oriented" solutions consisted essentially, and not surprisingly, of nothing more than subsidies for American-based banks that had been losing a lot of money in the region.[15] Help for the poor of Asia, whose world had been turned upside down and who could not hope to understand what was happening to them, was never forthcoming.

A quite dissimilar but just as jolting economic crisis occurred in Russia and Eastern Europe in 1998. The people in these countries were overtaken and impoverished by two dominant earthshaking factors: first, the gross corruption of the former Soviet system, which involved virtually turning over the assets of the economy, which had been mostly state-owned, to a select band of organized and often criminal interests; and second, after gross failures of an always poorly-administered privatization system imposed by the international financial community, there came a quite sudden insistence by international financial powers, primarily the IMF, that the Russians and East Europeans should bail themselves out of this crisis with "free market" policies and solutions. This insistence came in the wake of a devastating forty percent decline in the size of the Russian economy and a horrendous downturn in the standard of living during which poverty increased tenfold; the IMF and allied banking interests called for a grossly ill-advised "shock therapy" to relieve the situation. The IMF loan used to finance a recovery failed, and the people of Russia and the nearby nations, who had no say in accepting this loan and its terms, could hardly be considered culpable. Stiglitz is especially critical of "shock therapy" approaches.[16]

These prominent cases and several others—in Argentina, the Congo, Mexico, and varied locations—show the results of information deficits at both the policy-making level and within and amidst the milieu of ordinary citizens trying to deal with the economic facts of life as these are understood. It is little wonder that Stiglitz is concerned with such problems and that he has devoted three of his books and, significantly, a major portion of his Nobel Prize address to information deficits and policy-bungling as these affect developing areas of the world, harming the interests of the most vulnerable of peoples.

INIQUITOUS INEQUITIES, ESPECIALLY IN EQUITIES, AND THE PROBLEM OF OPAQUE MARKETS

The enormous U. S. burdens of record-level budget deficits, balance-of-payments shortfalls and trade deficits continue to be discussed and lamented even though few (and probably no) concrete correctives are being taken. The greatest awareness of the possibly severe short-term and long-term threats associated with deficit management is displayed by thoughtful analysts and critics in academia and occasionally in active politics and the civil service; but few of these individuals have access to any decision-making arenas of importance. This is one of the worst symptoms of an information deficit problem operating at many levels that must eventually be tackled, and sooner is always better than later. Less well-known, but also dangerous, are the secretive but harmful maneuvers associated with disruptions like the hedge fund crisis of 1999. The long shadow of this debacle still hangs over the U. S. and other major financial markets of the world because there is strong evidence that it could occur again. A large and mismanaged fund, the Long Term Capital Management Company, operating secretly and well below the regulatory radar, suddenly threw the financial establishment into a state of panic. LTCM has been characterized and analogized in the financial press as something like a dark asteroid, suddenly appearing out of nowhere to threaten a shattering of perhaps the entire world economy. The market atmosphere of mid-1999 quickly became a mad scene when instability raised its ugly head because of the machinations and mismanagement of LTCM, even though it represented only a small but very wealthy and highly-privileged group of investors. This apparently required a timely and effective bail-out of the firm by Federal Reserve Chairman Alan Greenspan, who held no apparent legal authority to come up with a solution.

Greenspan was able, all the same, to extract huge funding for the bail-out from fifteen institutions, including Citigroup, America's largest bank at the time, and Merrill Lynch, the largest stock brokerage firm. European "donors" as well were called upon to help LTCM. Greenspan was able to cobble together a fast $3.5 billion in order to save the hedge fund and its creditors. The costs of all of this to the smaller investors in the banks and brokerage houses were imposed suddenly, expensively, and arbitrarily. It was as if a heavy tax had been suddenly thrust upon them from out of the middle of nowhere. The explanation for the prompt reaction was that LTCM was simply "too big to fail."[17] The authorities sometimes take unprecedented, awkward, and odd ad hoc positions when it comes to matters of running the economy. One year later the somewhat less secretive Tiger Fund, also a hedge fund, went under after it had squandered billions of dollars.[18] The years 2001 and 2007 have also witnessed hedge fund crises and bankruptcies, and these have had bad rippling effects within the world's financial communities, especially Wall Street.

Secretive and exclusive hedge funds continue to operate without the benefits of regulation, and it is fair to say that they are not understood well to this day. How could they be? They operate well outside the parameters of public view. More than 8,000 of these funds are currently operating, and they manage well over $1 trillion in assets. They are highly-leveraged, speculative, and derivatives-oriented groups of investors. They operate without any regulation by national or international authorities even though they are capable of shaking up markets and governments around the globe. Their private and exclusive status accords tax advantages, which appear to greatly subsidize and benefit their executives and directors at the expense of the rest of us. Smaller and less exclusive hedge funds have come into being since 1999, and these also remain outside the public's view and, like their larger cousins, are excellent candidates for regulation. A very minimal regulation of these funds began in 2006 when the SEC set up a requirement of registration but with nothing else in the way of requirements or oversight. Hedge funds can and assuredly will continue to cause trouble for investors, the market, and the economies of America and the world. The typical entrance fee of one million dollars (though reduced in recent years in a few cases to only the bargain entrance fee of a quarter-million, perhaps a real bargain?) tells us that these are exclusive institutions, but that should hardly be an impediment to the cause of greater transparency. The life styles and expensive tastes of their officials have become the grist of Wall Street gossip. Reports of their often-questionable practices appear on a regular basis in the business press, and some market shake-ups are alleged to occur because of these funds.[19] One of the more recent concerns has been the intervention of these funds into currency markets, where their impact carries the potential for considerable destabilization.

The relevance of information economics to the peril-fraught LTCM hedge fund case is obvious enough. A financial institution, facing great troubles and even extinction, suddenly insinuates itself into the international economy where, despite its incompetence and its near-comeuppance, it is saved by extra-legal and certainly questionable means. The costs of this information deficit were great indeed for a wide range of economic actors, many or most of whom had never heard of Long Term Capital Management. The perils of the well past due-for-regulation hedge fund industry should no longer be thrust upon the public nor tolerated by it. Though Stiglitz does not go into the question of hedge funds in great detail,[20] it can be seen that there is a strong fit between this issue and the findings of information economics. Hedge fund information is purposely withheld and inaccessible; the conduct of their business, if much is found out about it, is shocking and crying for regulation; fairness is manifestly impossible in the absence of regulation and transparency; and the warts of what is called the "free enterprise" system becomes obvious, once more, for all of us to see and condemn. The venality of these institutions and the system that supports them was underscored when Amaranth, another large hedge fund, hit the wall in 2006. It was reported that the manager had "a fortune to gain—and little to lose" in the reckless gambles he had made with the assets of his clients.[21]

The first decade of the new century has also seen some ado about the new impacts of "private equity" and its effects upon markets. Many of these "private assets," of course, are in the hedge funds, but they are also tied to influential congregations of investors who go heavily with their assets into firms specializing in mergers, acquisitions, and hostile takeovers; they are also involved in the planning and presentation of IPO's (new offerings) that take place from time to time. (Access to IPO, initial public offering, investment is another fairly well-kept secret on Wall Street as far as many or most potential investors are concerned.) Most of the machinations involved with these processes are well outside the public's purview; the financial press and electronic media invariably learn of big and new deals after they have already been set into motion. As this is written we see still another massive blood-letting unfolding, at least figuratively, with a mortgage and credit crisis of unfathomable and certainly untold dimensions; and as in the past, we can put together at least one central fact: the institutions of Wall Street, combined with the negligence of Washington, are to blame. The case for the economics of information appears to apply to a host of considerations (as well as firms) on Wall Street but the typical investor operates, for the most part, very much in the dark. He or she must hope for a considerable amount of good luck. An old Wall Street saying tells us that an investor should hope that she or he is buying into the side of the equation that is doing the cheating. And even though such a claim, fairly typical within the investment community, may be flawed in some respects, it is obvious that many people who play the securities markets hold a cynical view of them.

INFORMATION DEFICITS OF LABOR, INVESTORS, CONSUMERS, AND OTHER STAKEHOLDERS

The need for information obviously arises in many policy and bargaining situations. The United Auto Workers appears to have been one of the first groups to be aware of this. This union was involved in a long strike in their industry during the post-World War II years over a demand that the companies should "open their books" to the accounting realities of the time and not just resort to perfunctory annual reports. This was an unprecedented campaign, but it was not successful in winning on this point; the problem still remains in bargaining over matters of wages, benefits, hours, and working conditions. Information deficits are also an acute problem for labor organizing, an area complicated by a marked and insufferable amount of mostly illegal foot dragging, clearly favoring the employer side. The well-documented law-breaking activities of companies faced with unionization include illegal firings, discrimination, demotions, promises of great and specific improvements if the workers forego union organization (a promise, which if made, is beyond the pale of the law), and threats of physical harm. This current state of affairs sets up routines carried out as though labor unions were never legalized in 1935 with a Wagner Act mandate that the government should not be neutral but instead, according to this Act's preamble, must encourage and support union organization as a matter of the public interest. But administration of labor law is now so out of hand that the criminality in vogue has spawned an industry of anti-union advisers and even lawyers who promote a multitude of violations; in some cases these people are authors of books counseling violation of various laws in order to prevent unionization. Professional ethical codes of the bar are of course ignored by such "consultants."[22]

This unjust set-up has been the major reason for the decline in unionization and the obvious political strength that might grow out of it. Legislative and administrative remedies are sorely needed, though merely enforcing the law would do much to change the balance in today's labor relations scene. It should be obvious that information deficits play an overwhelming role in this state of affairs. Merely spreading information about what constitutes legal or illegal conduct by the companies could make a contribution to fairness during most of these organizing efforts. No system of "free enterprise" as envisioned by Adam Smith or others can be said to exist here; instead we see something closer to the state of nature described by Rousseau or, far more likely, by Hobbes or Dickens' Mister Bumble. Adam Smith himself condemned greed, quite to the contrary of the purveyors of the myth that says such conduct would earn his endorsement.[23] Few employees are likely to know their legitimate and applicable rights in the union organization arena, and keeping such information from them, which is typically the choice of employers, calls the whole milieu of labor law and labor economics into question. Let us be clear, however, that information deficits are only a part of this severe problem. The inability of employees to do much to improve their position within labor-competitive atmospheres is also a basic part of the problem, and this is directly addressed by the information economists in a way that virtually removes any shred of legitimacy from the administration of these processes as these are currently carried out by the Bush Government and its appointees to the National Labor Relations Board.

The central role of information in any economic process underscores the relevance of the work of Stiglitz and his colleagues; but the knowledge deficits found in labor-management relations apply with almost equal force to the investment and consumer communities. The brokerage industry always knows more about financial markets than their typical investor-clients can hope to find out. Clients operate mostly on faith and hope for good luck even if they do manage to read a prospectus or other investment guides. The latest research suggests, as it always has, that a typical investor not only faces an information deficit, but is also incapable of making the kinds of investment decisions that are available to better-connected and much wealthier investors or institutions.[24] Anecdotal evidence of this problem, which greatly mounts over time, can be found in almost any issue of the *Wall Street Journal*, which provides us with article after article about brokers, financial managers and others who get into trouble by ignoring civil or criminal strictures of securities, banking, and other regulatory laws. A typical report of broker fraud may involve a routine of advising clients to buy a "thin" stock so that its price will rise quickly. The broker has of course already taken a position in this listing. When enough people have managed to push up the price in this way, the broker sells; and should the SEC monitors catch up with him, there will be penalties. Oddly and illogically the editorial page of this newspaper warns us, on a more or less continuous basis, that regulation of stock markets or of industries in general is unnecessary and even highly undesirable if we are to enjoy a smooth-running economy.

The most tragic shell games in the world of corporate managements over the past decade and a half—Enron, WorldCom, Tyco, Health South, Refco, AIG, Adelphi and others—precisely point once again to the issue of information access and availability. The accounting was wrong and surely misleading, and these corporations' operations were based upon deception.

The "anything goes" attitude of the Reagan years produced gross inequities in the securities markets, and the evidence points today to a revival of this period of merger mania. Mergers, acquisitions, and hostile takeovers dominated the financial news of the 1980s, allowing for quick profits, violations of the letter and spirit of antitrust laws, a wholesale degradation of stockholders' rights and interests, and some positively weird financial arrangements, such as a take-over of a relatively prosperous company by a bankrupt firm. Many or most of these takeovers were financed by high-premium bonds, also known as "junk bonds," or what critics dubbed "free money" for the take-over artists. "Junk bonds," according to an attorney who specialized in their issuance, "are like a tinderbox" for the economy.[25] This period also produced, perhaps to no discerning person's surprise, a record array of scandals, lawsuits, and belated criminal convictions that were typical of the corrupt Reagan era.

Small investors were required by these events to endure a period of what amounted to deregulation—in fact and in law—of the financial markets. Prosecutors were able, all the same, to snag some big movers and shakers and put them into golf course-style prisons. Michael Millken, the "junk bond king," was sent to prison while his brokerage firm, Drexel Burnham Lambert, went under. He did not appear to have much trouble there, in the flower garden city of Lompoc by the sea, though the authorities would not allow him to wear his toupee. The savings and loan scandal, one of the gravest the nation has ever faced, was also making headlines at this time. And Ivan Boesky, who invested in merger and buy-out "possibilities" that he had illegally been given advance knowledge about, paid a $100 million fine and went to prison shortly after giving one of his many speeches espousing and promoting "free enterprise."[26]

Despite its clouded and often shameful record, the combinatory urge is running rife once again. Bank mergers and takeovers have proceeded to a point at which some brokers and observers, perhaps seriously and perhaps not, are predicting that the U. S. will be down to only four banks in just a decade or two. And while this industry's scandals, executive games of musical chairs, outlandish salaries and perks, and reams of broken promises (one of the old saws of the American Bankers Association was that the savings from ATM installations would be passed along to customers, for example) have all helped to dominate the financial headlines. Meanwhile, the undoing of the Standard Oil case of 1910 has proceeded very far in the petroleum industry. Exxon has taken over Mobil, Chevron has married Texaco, and Conoco is now in bed with Phillips. Unocal was taken over by the Conoco-Phillips combine; but it has remained free to work, as it assiduously does, with the military dictators and human-rights violators of Burma. Gas prices have in the meantime become an important issue, but no worthwhile investigation of this phenomenon appears to be in the cards within the immediate future.

A race to merge utilities is also in the offing. Important protective legislation written in 1935 was rewritten by the infamous 107th Congress, and the public can expect to take a soaking as the rationale for utilities regulation, set out logically and forcefully by the Supreme Court in 1882, is abandoned. The victims of Enron's fraudulent rate-setting in California and other states in the 1990s are going to have company. The vagaries of utilities regulation, needless to say, are not susceptible to public input or concern on any scale commensurate to the importance of this issue. Small stockholders and certainly consumers should expect to be taken for a ride, and information deficits will play a major role in the unpromising picture that will soon emerge. The assumptions of the deregulation lobbyists that human nature has changed since the days when utility statutes and rulings had to be written to protect consumers and investors are, needless to say, patently false. Their case not only lacks any compelling need for change, but is additionally undermined by the questionable standards of corporate conduct found in America and the world.

In other corporate cases, most notably those of the drug and tobacco companies, the information gap has most seriously hinged upon product liability and careless product development, making the position of the consumer probably even more hapless than that of the investor. The murky and indeed seamy (and over-advertised) world of prescription drugs has now put consumers out of reach of the facts even more than in the past. Recent years have seen this industry indulging in false claims about imported drugs, conflicting claims about which drug is more effective for this or that malady, and this scene is complete with unprecedently shrill advertising suggesting to television audiences that they may be threatened by every conceivable problem from yellowing toenails to bad circulatory systems. New findings on the ineffectiveness of cholesterol treatments have undermined major revenue hopes of these companies. Drug lobbyists, we should be reminded, gave us a price-fixing system written into the 2004 Medicare revisions that few can really understand and which bear no conceivable relationship to any "free market" claim. This unbelievably bad legislation provides for a "doughnut hole," a period of years in which a person receives no benefits after having received them and before he or she will once again be eligible for them. Those who drafted this law have created the impression that they must have been insane. The credibility of the drug industry is apparently declining in tandem with America's health system and almost as fast as the lawsuits are piling up against it. The answer of the Bush Administration and its friends for this problem is simple enough: emasculate the Seventh Amendment, a measure strongly advocated by Thomas Jefferson and the Founders, and its protection of the right to sue. Many of the problems with drug prices, drug safety and medical care were begun or were intensified by the intrusion of profit seekers into Medicare in the 1990s, a significant and certainly unfortunate departure from the spirit of public trust and the original purposes of this important program. Today there is a great lack of information and understanding of the purposes and administration of Medicare, which is vital to this country's elderly population, which finds itself surfeited with television ads, competing claims, insurance company propaganda, and a Medicare explanation book issued by the government that is as confusing (and as pro-HMO) as it is thick.

Automobile industry recalls, insurance scams, the issue of obesity-causing foods, absurd industrial claims about the environmental sensitivities of the oil, lumber, and mining corporations, and deceptive practices about the origin of products have all been a part of the recent and contemporary opaque picture in consumer economics. Probably the most threatening portion of this landscape to consumers is finance. The "creativity" of the mortgage industry has produced millions in debt instruments of an inscrutable but certainly dubious character, such as adjustable-rate and interest-only loans. The decline of banking services alongside the increased charges for such services has caused a tremendous information deficit for the consumer to wade through. Foremost among these services, of course, are credit cards Usurious interest rates by historical or any other standards (up to 64 percent per year), a host of deceptive practices, and the continuously-revised and obscure "contracts" written in the smallest of type and the foggiest of prose possible make cardholders susceptible to horrendous costs and often bankruptcy. The newest legislation with regard to the latter was written by the card industry in 2005, and needless to say, the virtues of information economics are nowhere to be seen within its deliberately obscure terms. This industry has set unique records in many categories; but the most interesting one I have found is the practice of charging interest on debts already paid. (Much credit card legislation, in keeping with the morality of today, was literally written by lobbyists given unprecedented access to the floor of the House of Representatives.) Consumers often remain subject to criticism from loftier quarters for their failure to heed warnings or read their credit card contracts, just as they are characterized as antienvironmental and uncaring because they purchase vehicles or homes advertised with inflated and misleading claims; but most of these claims are reminiscent of the "buyer beware" mentality that held sway legally until 1906. Blaming victims is hardly ever an answer for any problem.

It is commonly averred that however important such issues may be, they can no longer be resolved within a national context. Globalization has proceeded to such a point, it is said, that its arena has taken over most, if not all, of the terms of debates and their resolution. International organizations like the WTO, the FTAA (Free Trade Area of the Americas, the successor to NAFTA), APEC, and certainly the IMF and the World Bank, as well as regional development banks and agencies, have superimposed their agendas upon many national-level economic matters. This remains a debatable supposition, however, and it may have even less relevance for a superpower like the United States.

But the Right, as we know, likes to shift arenas at their pleasure whenever it suits them; and that is why credit card law in America is neither federal nor international but state law. The card companies like Delaware, historically the leading favorite locale for incorporation, and they dearly love South Dakota, a state that has never bothered much with consumer protections nor with anything resembling fair interest rate levels. These are the two most prominent credit card incorporation locales and processing centers.

On the matter of which level of government is best to carry out this or that public policy, Stiglitz rejects at least some of the globalization rhetoric. He believes that national-level issues and decisions are relevant and important within their own context and on their own terms and he writes and speaks to these concerns, as one would expect, on a continuous basis. The simple truth is that each arena has some effects upon the others.[27]

STIGLITZ: EVER SEARCHING AND EMPHATIC

The works of Stiglitz published in the years since the Nobel triumph demonstrate an emphatic reiteration of his basic findings and premises. In his most recent book, in which he once again takes up the issues of globalization, he pointedly remarks that his "earlier academic work on the consequences of imperfect and limited information and imperfect competition led me to an awareness of the limitations of markets."[28] He then states that the deepest flaw in International Monetary Fund (IMF) policies and procedures is in that organization's "market fundamentalism," the belief that markets somehow—and all by themselves—lead to economic efficiency.[29] And there is a note of triumph, as well as of reason and deep understanding, in his statement that "Today, by and large, there is (at least among economists, if not among politicians) an understanding of the limits of markets. The scandals of the 1990s in America and elsewhere brought down 'Finance and Capital American Style' from the pedestal on which they stood for too long."[30] His work emphasizes that the short-term and shortsighted approach of Wall Street to economic affairs is increasingly seen as antidevelopment because it ignores the necessary long-term thinking and planning required if we are ever to successfully assist the poor countries while building and reforming the world's interdependent economy.[31]

Stiglitz has also taken umbrage at the economics discipline's continued insistence upon using outmoded measures, though he is certainly not the only critic disgusted with its sadly lacking statistical regime. The gross domestic product, he points out, is an obvious example; this measure ignores two major factors contributing to an economy's health: depreciation of physical assets and the cost of environmental destruction. GDP factors in the growth when scarce oil reserves are used, but it provides no accounting of the long-term effects of such activity. Replacing gross domestic product (GDP) with such a measure, which could be quite capably established, might reframe our focus and make us appreciate our long-term interests. This is certainly not a new issue, but it is well past time to be doing something about it.[32] It can be concluded that Stiglitz and his colleagues have not only fostered a shake-up and stocktaking for traditional economics, but that they also seek to remedy its basic methods, measures, and assumptions.

A POLITICAL, SOCIAL AND HISTORICAL CONTEXT FOR INFORMATION ECONOMICS

The landmark article providing a basic explanation of information economics, accompanied by suitable and impressive proofs, first appeared in 1986.[33] This was a time, of course, when the Reagan Administration, though it was running headlong into scandal after scandal, including the unconstitutional and shocking activities of Iran-Contra, was still riding high and was still seeking to effect a consensus on economic thought that can only be considered very remote from the scientific approaches, outlooks, and findings of the information economists. This was hardly a propitious time for the appearance of a revolutionary assault upon the established wisdom or the established order, and the proof of this can be inferred in the grossly underwhelming attention given to these findings. Stiglitz and his colleagues were almost never seen in any popular media, which to this day continue to extol the no-longer-living "free enterprise system." This remarkable scholarship was widely ignored, perhaps most especially within the caverns of the economics discipline, which has functioned largely on a continuing business-as-usual basis; information economics is not only ignored within the normal (and often normative) routines of conferences as well as in the production of books and academic journal articles. We are quite remarkably still awaiting the day when Stiglitz or his colleagues or their information paradigm merits even a mention within the pages of any of the basic micro or macro textbooks (though it must be admitted that there is a modicum of acceptance in the texts devoted to development economics.)[34]

This state of affairs—one in which we can assert that almost nothing is happening within the economics discipline that could even be generously termed a response (except perhaps for a few matters like the appearance of the volume organized in honor of Stiglitz)[35]—is mirrored by events in the "real world," where Stiglitz is observed as an occasional guest speaker or occasional contributor of an op-ed newspaper article or perhaps, even less likely, as a guest on a television news program. In none of these instances is it likely that there will be any mention of information economics; the media are probably more interested in his views on issues such as disaster relief for the poor countries or, perhaps, the minimum wage. Stiglitz is never presented as the man who disproved the "free enterprise" thesis, much as this needs to be done. Pondering this, one of my graduate students offered that, in his opinion, the media has simply "stiffed him" and can be expected to continue to do this. These institutions are guilty, in his opinion, of deliberate omission and deception. Even the Nobel Prize story of 2001 was handled quietly, though this is often the case with many of these awards.

In searching for an historical context for a new awareness of information economics, then, it must be admitted that for the moment there is little or no apparent context at all. We can complain about this, but it may have little effect. The story of the collapse of "free enterprise" and its replacement with a thoughtful new paradigm is, apparently, not seen as a story at all. We must await further developments, as some like to say.

We can, however, find and analyze historical events that can or may give some kind of shape or direction—or, at the very least, a background—for these findings. Such a task compels us to pick and choose somewhat arbitrarily from among these as a matter of expeditious necessity, but it is certainly possible to extract from recent decades the kind of informative happenings that may ultimately give and prove some real context for information economics and the new pathways in which it is developing.

"Free enterprise," as we all know, is a phrase most likely to be uttered by the political practitioners found in conservative and rightist domains—places perhaps like Republican gatherings or "think tank" meetings in which various meandering speakers continue, quite thoughtlessly, to mouth the old platitudes over and over. (It is assumed, of course, that we must always be hesitant and careful when seeking to explain ideological matters and terms, but there is often no other practical way in which to subject some of these topics and ideas to analysis.) Perhaps it is fair to assume that conservative political parties provide the most receptive and maybe even enthusiastic forums for "free enterprise" assertions and myth-celebration. What has happened to such parties in the advanced economies of the world, and particularly within the Western orbit, can therefore instruct and guide us towards the context we seek.

In the main these parties have accepted the welfare state—social security systems, national health schemes, protections for labor unions, consumers, and cooperatives, housing programs, minimum wages, and supports of various kinds for the poor, elderly, and disabled—into their programs, platforms, and governance. There are obviously variations within these different societies—France, for example, has opted for a thirty-five hour workweek—but it is safe to say that, with the occasional hesitation here or a slightly different ruffle or flourish there, there is a broad acceptance of programs—and, to a limited extent, even a rather pragmatic ideology—similar to the New Deal in America, or to go to what may be the other extreme, the very extensive welfare systems of France, Germany, or Sweden.

The major exceptions to this are the conservative parties of the United States, Britain, Japan, and Australia. The future of Australia's major party of the right, the Liberals, is somewhat in doubt after the country's voters ditched them in a landslide defeat in late 2007. Even after many years of John Howard, the longtime Liberal Prime Minister, a considerable portion of the nation's welfare state remained intact.[36] Had Howard, a real class warrior in the style of George W. Bush, managed to hang on, the social protections Australia had known for much more than half a century might very well have been taken away. The British Conservatives and the Republicans in America have quite obviously been less successful lately than in recent decades. The elections of 2006, despite increasingly tight restrictions on voting aimed at Democrats, minorities, and the poor, wiped out the Republican majorities in the Congress, and at this writing the Democrats also appear strong for the elections, whether presidential or congressional, to be held in the near future. (Recent elections in the U. S. require that we add the proviso that they must be fair.) Opinion polling of younger age groups shows that their likely voters' tastes do not bode well for the Republicans at all, since these appear more supportive of welfare state measures while simultaneously appearing much less concerned about divisive social issues concerned with religion, race, or gay rights.

Scanning the world is always a useful and worthwhile enterprise, though it is fraught with possibilities for error, but conservatism appears to be in decline almost everywhere. The Conservative Party of Britain suffered an ignominious landslide defeat in 1997 at the hands of Tony Blair and his "new" Labour Party, which has been successful enough since then to continue to hold office. (Labour, however, has suffered some significant losses in national and local elections recently and it is currently not doing well in the polls, largely because of its support of Bush's Iraq War.) The Tories may be hard-pressed to replace Labour in the next election, but they could be successful because of Blair's obviously mistaken approach to foreign policy and defense issues. But if the Tories win, it will be a victory of a party constituted quite differently than in the past in terms of its approach to the welfare state. The Conservatives have gone out of their way to denounce and renounce Thatcherism, the disastrous anti-welfare shtick that served them well for a time—a time now well past. They have made it plain that if they are successful, they will not basically threaten welfare state programs, they will not push for privatization as they have in the past, and they will not try to bash the unions, which was one of Prime Minister Margaret Thatcher's favorite pastimes. They wish, in other words, to win elections.[37]

For its part the Labour Party, despite its foreign policy and defense reversals and the loss of much of its Socialist zeal over the years, has nonetheless maintained the welfare state in a quite responsible way. Blair made up his mind, early on, that there would be no wholesale cuts in programs and there would also be limits (though probably too few of these) on privatization; for guidance he only had to look at the disasters of Thatcher in these spheres.[38] And the results are impressive: the British poverty rate is less than half that of America, where the Bush-led drive for privatization, which has also raised its ugly head at the state levels, has had considerable success. Helping the poor in the British way, according to another leading American economist, Paul Krugman of Princeton University, is a superior approach to the misguided work that Bush and the Republicans have been trying to carry out in the United States.[39]

All of this means that, for the moment at least and probably for a long time into the future, the Republicans in America and the Liberal Democratic Party governments of Japan will be the only significant forces left in the world among the wealthier nations who deny the efficacy and worthwhile character of the welfare state. It is not an encouraging atmosphere, to say the least, for the world's conservative dinosaurs.

The welfare state must be the trip wire issue in this analysis because it is the natural state of affairs—the natural home, so to speak—that can accommodate the economics of information and its political ramifications. The political context we seek, then, is set before us by the machinations and, more precisely, by the evolution of political parties found in advanced industrial societies, the wealthy nations of the world, and the message they provide is clear: the policies and programs of a pre-welfare state or post-welfare state milieu simply *do not fit* the aspirations of citizens. One reason for this, it is reasonable to assume, is that the enamored view of "free enterprise" some parties have taken in the past prevents them from dealing with reality; but just as importantly, parties and politicians are required by this same reality to move in the direction of the welfare state and against the limitations some may seek to impose upon it with schemes for privatization or deregulation (or, in some cases, denationalization.)

This analysis acknowledges that the parties historically favoring welfare state measures have made policy and ideological adjustments over the years. British Labour, for example, long ago gave up Clause Four of its Manifesto, which called for large-scale nationalization of the economy.

The Democratic Party, especially under the leadership of President Bill Clinton, took what it considered a more pragmatic approach towards the welfare state though critics, including Stiglitz and this author, believe that this was unnecessarily overdone.

Even with this slight concession in our argument, it remains the case that conservative parties in the industrialized countries have largely, except for the Republicans (stay tuned), incorporated the welfare state and its protections into their programs or, on the other hand, have chosen ideological and policy stands that are markedly unsuccessful.

This reality, much like the almost total lack of awareness of information economics, has yet to be appreciated in the United States, which will hopefully and eventually catch up with the rest of the world. It is certainly and shamefully the case at present that much of our political dialogue proceeds with some ideas still abroad about doing away altogether with Social Security, Medicare, housing, nutrition, education, and public assistance programs. It is not recognized that the times are changing and that the major spokesperson for this kind of claptrap, George W. Bush, will soon be heading for Texas. He has managed to insure that the conservative case cannot be sustained much longer; and election results and opinion polls are now pointing decidedly against the Right, whether one's view is short-term or long-term. Their majorities were always narrow; now they appear to be gone, perhaps for good.

PLACING THE ECONOMICS OF INFORMATION WITHIN THE FRAMEWORK OF THE DISCIPLINE'S EVOLUTION

Where does the economics of information fit within the framework of the discipline? In other words, what does the economics of information mean to economics? It does not fit particularly well into the structure of the discipline if we are to believe that the introductory micro and macro textbooks should be our guides. Stiglitz and his colleagues receive virtually no attention and no credit for their work, though they make a small dent in the texts devoted to economic development. Relatively few papers are read at economics, political science, sociology, or any other conferences on the subject, and exploring its applications has been left largely to a coterie of scholars in America and abroad who are obviously peculiar enough to take this up.

It could be argued that this is the case with many branches and schools of economics or other disciplines; the world is made up, after all, of broad vistas for inquiry. This leaves us all in an odd position, surely, for the domain of general observers is the one ultimately taking up the works of scholars and translating them, however crudely, into an eventually-arrived-upon consensus which may or may not accurately reflect the contributions of social science. In the case at hand, the economics of information, it can be safely assumed that, comparatively speaking, its light remains under a bushel while the legions of "free enterprise" minions continue to mislead the public and themselves on a whole raft of questions (see Appendix C).

The question of the place of the economics of information within the discipline remains. So where can we start? Has the economics of information had, or should it have, as broad an effect on our thinking, for example, as Keynes' work on government spending, taxes, interest rates, and economic recovery? Many might argue that it should not. Keynes came along at an appropriate time, a ghastly time for many people, with nothing less than an earth-shattering set of analyses and prescriptions, and his work informed many of the policies and solutions of Franklin D. Roosevelt's New Deal Administration. All of this resulted in heaps of credit, and sometimes blame, on both Keynes and Roosevelt. (One of the stranger sideshows of the past half-century, often given voice, featured the claim that Lord Keynes was a rabid Socialist, which was hardly the case.) If there is any drama to be found within economics, it certainly can be said to have played itself out in the fiscal policies and recovery programs of the 1930s, and these amounted to what can only be called a peaceful but definite revolution.

But if a large-scale revolution is indeed what is needed to establish the credentials of a noted thinker, how much bigger can the issue be than the exposed and mistaken fraud of "free enterprise"? Have we not been drowning for decades if not centuries in its announced virtues and alleged certainties about some kind of long-term economic justice? Is it not the case that its imminent removal from the lexicon of the discipline's terminology most certainly amounts to a revolution, even one of earthshaking importance? Just think of the revisions that apparently are in order as a result of the labors of Akerlof, Spence, and Stiglitz and their colleagues! If Adam Smith or Friedrich Hayek or Ludwig Von Mises were alive today, this would be a time of "back to the drawing boards" for them (see Appendices C and D). The premises of many a tome, article, essay, or editorial would have to be reexamined. In the case of magazines and journals like *Weekly Standard,*

National Review, or *Reason*, any task undertaken, for example, in the cause of removing or recasting the phenomenon of "free enterprise" for the volumes they have produced over the years would require a forbidding mountain of revision and, in many or most cases, excisions filling dustbin after dustbin.

The Nobelists of 2001 will eventually exceed even the force and power of the great Keynes. Much will occur, we have the right to expect, after more reading and thinking have been carried out. But what, one might ask, of those who have developed theoretical work based in part upon the contributions of the great Cambridge don? Where might they fit within the various rankings we are pondering in this small and temporary exercise of strata, data, and fun?

With time and space limitations to consider, it will be necessary to look at only a few who have managed to make some kind of overall impact upon economics and, at least tangentially, upon public consciousness. The Laffer Curve people, though they are hardly a deserving group, leap first to mind. These are the ones who deftly honed their version of Keynes—working not from the government revenue side, but from the market side, better known today as the "supplyside"—to bring about fiscal policy "axioms" proved to be impressive as far as President Ronald Reagan and other conservatives were concerned. They believed, with Keynes, that policy could translate into an economic stimulant. In a nutshell, this school of thought believed that cutting taxes by a certain amount could, indeed would, create such a flurry of private-sector spending—on both the investment and consumption sides—that it would lead to greater revenues for the government than would have been the case without a tax cut.

There is logic at work here. The major problem is finding the point on the Laffer Curve at which revenue losses will be minimized while a tax cut stimulus is maximized; and alas, this is not such an easy point to find. The massive Reagan deficits, set in record-breaking numbers that would only be surpassed in the George W. Bush years, were the unfortunate policy failure and result. President Reagan himself was so taken and so twitterpated with this proposition that he even claimed on a couple or more occasions that the more taxes were cut, the more revenue government will realize. We are still financing the massive debts of those unenlightened years. And, just for the record, Reagan was no great tax-cutter, either. His later years saw recognition that tax increases were indeed needed and justified.

A constant stream of research has shown, unfortunately for the heavily ideological crowd, that it is difficult for the Laffer Curve phenomenon to really work out. The most recent test, of course, is found in the tax cuts for the rich that George W. Bush and his Republican Congress authorized at the beginning of his years in office. Peter Orszag of the Congressional Budget Office has provided what appears to be most recent verification of this sad tale; he says that these cuts had virtually no traceable expansionary effect for the economy.[40] The plain truth is that it is difficult to realize the promised miracle of revenue growth. It appears highly unlikely, then, taking this research into consideration, that the "supplyside" approach deserves much of our attention and in my opinion there is no reason to have any special feelings of gratitude towards it. To their credit, some of the early advocates of "supplyside" perspectives have abandoned ship. The Laffers may have borrowed a couple of ideas from Keynes in a backhanded way, but it cannot reflect any of his glories.

There are other contributions, of course, that have managed to make their mark. We should not overlook those who have blended psychology to give us insights on market behavior and/or responses to a variety of stimuli. It is also claimed by a small group that "Rubinomics," named for Bill Clinton's Treasury Secretary, has helped us to understand the importance of education and training in developing jobs and a competitive position in the world (though many of us held this view intuitively anyway.) How this precisely works with Rubin's other remedies for globalization pressures, such as the NAFTA Treaty he nurtured and promoted, is not clear to any number of writers and observers, including myself. He is a deficit hawk, and this is a point well-taken nowadays by many of us.

This is a mere scratching of the surface, but it is fair to ask how many theorists and scholars in economics have had as great an impact (already) as the 2001 Nobelists; the answer is that there are few, if any, and probably none at all; the passage of time and the development of understanding promise a demonstration that this is the case.

ANTICIPATING THE RESPONSE OF THE RIGHT: SEMANTICS AND INFORMATION ECONOMICS

It should probably be assumed that there is no conspiracy on the Right aimed at simply ignoring the findings of information economics for a number of practical reasons. First and foremost among these is that the concepts of asymmetric bargains and an obvious information lack on at least one side of a deal are easy to grasp; even the thickest ideologue should therefore be able to discern that there is something there. Certainly the day will arrive—it has already occurred in one minor case—when a columnist or editor of perhaps even an academic will realize that there is a real problem here that must somehow be addressed. Those who then find no arrows in their quiver may choose to argue that this is merely a semantic distinction.

Such an alleged distinction could be based upon the patently false charge that a defense of market economics—as opposed to a "free enterprise system"—is still viable and that a simple change in term usage will do the trick so that we can all proceed down the same old trail as before. There are many problems with such an assertion, however, because it is readily answered by anyone wishing to refer to the Nobel Prize Speech or, perhaps more specifically, to the 1986 landmark article which charts this finding in quite cogent and easily-understood language. Though a few sub-points are set out in the Speech and in the article, a reader who centers upon the no-longer-valid claim that markets more or less automatically clear in a Pareto-efficient way should be able to smell the coffee and appreciate that it is time indeed for the defenders of the old system to see that the cause of market economics needs to be quickly and effectively reassessed. This is not the end of their world, after all (except perhaps for the Ayn Rand fanatics); they can go on to other subjects that may fit better with their ideological lifestyles or, perhaps better still, take up painting with pastel water colors.

SOME NOTES ON THE NOBEL PRIZE IN ECONOMICS

The Nobel Prize in Economics is obviously one of the great landmarks of recognition for the scholars associated with the economics of information. There is, alas, the more than occasional detractor found within the discipline itself who holds that this award amounts to very little indeed; and so, with some reluctance, I take up the defense of this Prize as well as the great work of the three 2001 Nobelists. Many economists like to point out, as indeed some noneconomists do, that the late Alfred Nobel, the Swedish magnate who made his fortune selling dynamite and other commodities, forbade having any of these well-known prizes used to honor social scientists. Some might consider this unfair; I certainly do. Social sciences cannot claim the great precision found in physics or biochemistry or mathematics; but they are sciences, all the same, because they employ scientific method—including the basic methods mandate of hypothesis, testing, and proof—and discoveries in all of the social sciences can be shown to have advanced the knowledge and understanding of humankind. New frontiers in economics and political science are today being established, and some of these, I would assert, hold great promise.

In the 1960s some activists in the International Economic Association worked with the Bank of Sweden to set up a Nobel Prize. The award bears the name of Nobel because it is awarded in his honor. There seems to be no real objection to provision of the award in this way; the real objection that I have most encountered over the years is based upon the few occasions when a Nobel laureate is honored for proving that the work of a prior Nobelist is demonstrably wrong. Why, they ask, was the first award made when it could be proved so wrong? There seems to be no way to avoid such juxtapositions, however, when it is remembered that economics has been unable, to date at least, to master its domain in the way that the "hard" sciences do. But those sciences, of course, also have had long histories during which some great landmark discovery of a Newton, for example, is overtaken by the work of an Einstein. There is no reason, however, to eliminate awards and recognition (nor, for that matter, to alter our esteem for Newton, whose great work has largely held up). Science should honor its best work, and the awards received are a part of the tradition and rhythms of its progress and evolution.

4

Globalization: *The* Pressing Economic Issue

> . . . while the commitment to a particular ideology deprived countries of the choices that should have been theirs, it also contributed strongly to their failures.
>
> —Joseph E. Stiglitz, *Globalization and Its Discontents*, p. 221

> If a free society cannot help the many who are poor, it cannot save the few who are rich.
>
> —John F. Kennedy, Inaugural Address, January 20, 1961

EXTENDING THE STIGLITZ ANALYSIS: CRITIQUING THE INTERNATIONAL VERSION OF "TRICKLE-DOWN" ECONOMICS

Adam Smith's "invisible hand" formula, as modified by the depression-era contributions of John Maynard Keynes, has guided international economic policy since the end of World War II. There have been occasional departures, as one might expect, such as the fixed currency trading arrangements set up by the Bretton Woods Agreement of 1947; but these are largely treated by economic historians as temporary expedients. A longer-lasting and much more significant departure has occurred in the case of agricultural subsidy policies of the Western nations, depriving producers in the poor countries the consideration and fairness they need and deserve. Critics of Smith's adherents point to such corruptions of the "pure" Smithian model as evidence of hypocrisy and selfishness, of course, but while such points can be easily and at times even usefully employed against conservative and right-wing economic and political forces and their apologists, these critics have rarely bothered with, and are mostly unaware of, the delicate but carefully-constructed—and totally devastating—critique Stiglitz and his associates have provided. They would do well to study it.

Faith in the "invisible hand" formula, Stiglitz believes, invariably fosters trickle-down economics,[1] a term seldom used by its practitioners even though it has dominated American politics at least since the retrograde years of the Reagan era. These practitioners prefer to sugarcoat the formula by employing other emphases, such as "supply-side economics," the "free market," "savings accounts" (a favorite when health care or Social Security issues are raised, as though the answer for such needs can by met by individual savings efforts of a middle class facing one attack after another on its assets by the multinational corporations and the privileged echelons of the economy), "individual initiative," "states' rights" (unless state governments wish to support progressive measures for the education, or perhaps the environment), and always the much-abused concept of "incentives." They rarely try to explain the basics of the trickle-down approach despite their strong support for it.

This approach says that the prosperity of all can best be assured by policy measures used to strengthen the wealthiest tiers of the economic ladder by freeing them from the problems of taxation and regulation. Inevitably, this assumption states or implies, the wealthy will enhance the welfare of all of us because they will loosen up and spend their earnings and capital on investments, leading to job creation, money in the pockets of consumers, and innovations in efficiency, technology, marketing, and even philanthropy. Trickle-down economics requires great faith in corporations and the rich, which invariably proves to be misplaced, and it also presupposes that they should be in control of the important investment and spending decisions that govern all of our lives. Anyone who takes a long view of economics, we are advised, will realize that economic activities carried out by whomever are a given; so in a certain sense it does not matter whether tax cuts or subsidies are given to the rich, to middle income people, or to the poor, because none of these groups can be expected to sit on their bank accounts. The only question, given this information, is where economic assets should be initially placed. Trickle-down opponents are likely to emphasize the dynamics of consumer purchasing power and the necessity of good wage levels, for which there is ample empirical support, as well as a need for certain types of regulation, but such persons are sometimes asked to concede that, in the long run, it may not matter where incentives are initiated. The short answer to such an assertion is that the world provides much more dodgy sets of economic factors than are apparently perceived by the questioner; but it is also the case that moral considerations should be allowed into policy-making—giving the least well-off a better set of advantages, for example—under these circumstances (and, I would add, under many other circumstances as well.)

Keynes would have never conceded that it does not matter where tax advantages or public policies are placed or begun. His seemingly flippant answer to this is that in the long run we are all dead, but what he was really saying, certainly, is that social and political factors as well as a little thought will tell us that the question of *who* administers and allocates scarce capital resources is an all-important consideration that has a great deal to do with the question of who will benefit from policies and who will yield political as well as economic power.

Applications of trickle-down economics to the international sphere can and should be construed as basically farcical and fraudulent attempts to manage and consolidate economic and political power. The international economy since 1945 should be characterized as "trickle-down with a vengeance" because foreign policy is always weighed down by political considerations. Thoroughly and astonishingly corrupt political figures—Pinochet, Marcos, Mobutu Sese-Seko, Suharto—have profited to the tune of millions and even billions of dollars from American aid, trade, and political concessions of various kinds because it was believed that these leaders were politically dominant, anticommunist, and acceptable enough from an economic standpoint so that they could be relied upon to see that the trickle-down processes would actually trickle down.[2] Costly political as well as economic losses for the U. S. proved to be the result as these pooh-bahs interpreted American support as an endorsement for their regimes of murder, torture, the stifling of dissent, kleptocracy, and what can only be termed gross economic inefficiency. (It must be noted that some of the greatest caterwauling in support of such governments came from the conservative and "free enterprise"-oriented economists who advised them in exchange for good fees. Well-known names associated with conservative economics and causes were directly involved with the fascistic governments of Chile, Indonesia, and the Philippines, among others.[3])

The trickling down claptrap, as policy or as process, is bad enough when it occurs within the loose and sympathetic boundaries of American politics. But with virtually no legal constraints in the various Third World environments in which it has been employed, the results have been as unconscionable as they are counterproductive. Suharto-era practices in Indonesia, to cite an acute example, included police accosting any just-fired employee at the door of the factory, while the Marcos regime seized peasant lands without compensation in the Philippines. (He turned some of these over to an American-based pineapple and banana company.) Wage rates in Honduras' garment factories remain less than a dollar a day, and it is fair to point out that any and all regimes in that country have labored heavily under the sway of U. S. interests. And child labor, an institution wedded to systems which seem to invariably meet the demands of the trickle-downers, persists to this day in many or most Third World economies.

The IMF and World Bank bureaucracies, Stiglitz points out, have been very much one and the same with the basic approaches used in the administration of U. S. aid. They have believed and practiced their faith, against all the evidence, that heavy-handed elite forces in the recipient nations could be trustworthy and amenable to a market awareness informed mostly by common sense (and probably some Milton Friedman-admiring advisers). So, despite the heavy costs of reactionary policies, corruption, and too often, brutality as well, societies in Asia, Africa, and Latin America have been forced to manage their way through currency crises, inflationary prices, shortages, widespread privation, crop failures, disease, and other calamities with the "help" of this type of leadership. These leaders and elites are also expected to emphasize building up exports, repayment of debt, and above all, belt-tightening measures for the masses, all in the cause of running a tight economic ship. A basic problem in working with this set of injunctions is that the kind of economic groundwork envisioned by Adam Smith has never been achieved in these countries, but this glaring deficiency is slighted or ignored.

Management of foreign economies by the U. S. and by agencies such as the IMF and World Bank is summarized by Stiglitz as (1) a conscious implementation of the "invisible hand" concept as set out by Smith, (2) a failure to administer programs in ways that would align these with Smith's format and ideals, and (3) finally, a failure to realize that Smith's thought, in all events, is inapplicable and, to put it bluntly, just plain wrong.[4] The saddest part of this litany is found, needless to say, in the massive human suffering that has been the result. This is no mere intellectual quibble; this is a debate that has been resolved into adverse social consequences for millions of peoples.

It must be agreed that some countries—Argentina, Brazil, India, and Vietnam are examples—have managed to improve their lot over the past decade or so despite all of the handicaps faced by developing nations, and critical observers will most certainly claim that such gains have been made in spite of, rather than because of, IMF, World Bank, and WTO policies. Whatever the case, the world economy may be less vulnerable than it was in the late 1990s. Some increases in representation within the councils of these organizations are now being worked out, and this is some kind of minor achievement for these countries and for organizations such as the Fund.[5] The ability of a few countries to improve their economies and to join into the world trading system is a signal indicator of their efforts and, perhaps as well, of the supporting efforts they have received from abroad. Many of the world's nations, it is plain, are still left behind, and this is notably the case with African countries. There can be little question that these countries have often been ignored and that any number of them are found at the bottom of the list in terms of any hope of wealth or growth.

AID, TRADE, AND DEVELOPMENT—MANY VOICES OF SUPPORT, BUT ONLY A MODICUM OF PROGRESS

International commerce also has a unique way of creating problems when they did not exist before; a significant barrier to peace, growth, and progress, according to Amy Chua, is an intensification of strife in developing countries between ethnic groups, especially when some groups are identified within the culture (as in Brazil, Indonesia, Mexico, the Philippines, and certainly the Middle East, among other places) as traditionally "better off."[6] These rivalries usually bring corruption into administrative and policy equations. Corruption is naturally deemed a major obstacle to both trade and aid, but it sometimes grows and spreads with various forms of encouragement from multinational corporations, international institutions such as the IMF and the World Bank, and even the United Nations. It seems at times to appear at every turn in the development process, whether we look at banking practices and loan policies, contracting, governmental administration, or even, sad to say, within some non-governmental organizations (NGOs). It is ubiquitous within the developing world—Central America, for example, but also India, Indonesia, Nigeria, Zambia, Zimbabwe, and a host of other countries. It is a dispiriting sight to behold, as this writer can vouch from many unfortunate personal experiences in Asia; and the weight of corruption on the economic systems of these nations is immeasurably heavy.

Then, too, we have the nay-sayers, an unhelpful group believing that no amount of economic assistance can ever be successfully administered. George Easterly is one of the most-quoted holders of this view, and it should be pointed out and admitted that he is skillful in providing a fair measure of data for his case.[7] Many Peace Corps veterans, however, to cite a noteworthy source to the contrary, would dispute his findings. And though no literature review can really exhaust all of the tendencies, claims and opinions one might cull from this list, there remains, of course, the unto ward but very large amount of materials continuing to posit the dated distractions of the neoclassical argument with its irrelevant assumptions and descriptions.[8]

The consensus on these matters, we can be reasonably sure, is that international trade is a given and that we must all support this cause however we define it or tinker with it, while aid, in virtually any form—grants, loans, technical assistance, or whatever—is necessary as well if the world's poor are ever to participate in the international economy and enjoy a better standard of living and, just as importantly, realize and possess any hope for their futures.

This does not move us far analytically; but Stiglitz has his own take on these issues, informed by his basic contribution of information economics, which has a broader set of applications in this sphere than may be generally appreciated. His approach calls upon empiricism as well as a dollop of common sense. The empiricism is naturally connected to his academic training; and his common sense, one must expect, has something to do with his life experiences in the smog-ridden and forbidding city of Gary.

The Stiglitz critique of the international economic order therefore rests primarily upon the priority he invariably accords to science. His observations of various economic crises—most notably in the cases involving Russia, Argentina, and East Asia in the last years of the last century—include, most directly, his critiques of the assumptions made by the International Monetary Fund and the World Bank. These assumptions have been almost always soaked in ideology, derived in many of the same ways as the assumptions drawn from the classical formulas about the American economy.

The mystique of market forces has been paramount and transcendent in these two organizations, and their insistence upon ideology has been so strong that they are intent upon trying the same old formulas, Stiglitz notes, even when their experiences have shown them that they are bound to fail. We occasionally hear that one definition of insanity is to continue with the same course of action despite failure piled upon failure; but Stiglitz documents, as will be seen, that this has most certainly been the case with both the IMF and the World Bank.

Far too often, the issues of international trade are characterized in the popular and business press as essentially divided into "acceptance" and "nonacceptance" of globalization; alternatively, there are statements or allusions suggesting a contest between "free trade" and "protectionism." But no one, least of all the large multinational corporations based in the U. S., Bermuda, the British Virgin Islands, or elsewhere, believes that trading rivals should be allowed to wreak havoc upon the domestic economy. Safeguards can be the only available path for an economy involved, first and foremost, in its own preservation. The "free trade" argument, often tied to the politics of the Right and today to the policies of the Bush Administration, is still being stridently made even in the face of enormous and threatening balance-of-payments and trade deficits and their accompanying administrative and management problems. Continuing to heed this catechism could prove to be a severe blow to our national security. The U. S. trade deficit has now surpassed seven percent of the gross national product, and no workable initiatives to deal with this problem (other than rhetoric) have been proposed by the Executive Branch. The long-term integrity of public finance, debt instruments, and the dollar are at stake, and "free enterprise" is often the basic and lame answer offered as the cure.

Specific formulas are offered from time to time with the implication that these will provide practical and workable answers to the problem. For many years in the 1980s and early 1990s, for example, various ratios of dollar-to-yen values were suggested as salvation for the problems of the Japanese trade surplus and the U. S. trade deficit. These ratios, sadly, failed to materialize in many cases, or if they did, they invariably failed to address the problem. Today the idea of the over-valued yuan is blamed as a basic cause of the deficit problem, but many or most observers appear skeptical about the hope for revaluation of this currency and the supposed benefits this might bring. The current Treasury Secretary, Henry M. Paulson, Jr., makes frequent trips to China, but nothing in this relationship appears to change in any substantial way.

EXPLAINING AND MEETING THE PROBLEMS CAUSED BY GLOBALIZATION

> We are no longer writing the rules of interaction among separate national economies. We are writing the constitution of a single global economy.
>
> —Renato Ruggiero, the first Director-General of the World Trade Organization, 1995[9]

It is not difficult to discern which political and economic issue area receives the most attention from Stiglitz. His career has placed him at the forefront in urging and challenging the world to deal with poverty, its major problem, and undoubtedly a root cause of many other problems. His time at the World Bank and with the Council of Economic Advisers brought him face-to-face with the forces and many of the personnel responsible for dealing with this multifaceted set of concerns. His frequent appearances and presentations in international forums, and especially those made at the decision-making centers (like the World Trade Organization, the IMF, and the World Bank) pertinent to this set of issues, demonstrate his acknowledged role as one of the leading experts on globalization and most of the economic issues raised by this phenomenon. Stiglitz has contributed three books to this subject: *Globalization and Its Discontents, Fair Trade for All: How Trade Can Promote Development* (with Andrew Charlton),[10] and *Making Globalization Work.* And to belabor this point further, he is entirely consistent in his policy preferences and in the advice and demands he makes upon international organizations, the world community, and most emphatically, upon the leaders of the rich nations.

Stiglitz has quite naturally demonstrated several other major concerns and has written about a great variety of political economy topics, and these are taken up in books and articles addressing these subjects. His books include *The Roaring Nineties: A New History of the World's Most Prosperous Decade,* a critique of the policies of the Clinton years; *Towards a New Paradigm in Monetary*

Economics, coauthored with Bruce Greenwald,[11] his major attempt to delve into this policy thicket; and *Whither Socialism?*,[12] an examination of this concept at a time when Stiglitz, as well as a supposed world consensus, have held that experiments in promoting equality, at least of the state-sponsored kind, are coming to an end. He writes that we can learn, all the same, from the issues raised by this idea's sunset and make adjustments to economic systems, certainly to the various welfare state measures and programs, in light of these findings. This latter work was written well before recent elections in Argentina, Bolivia, Brazil, Chile, Ecuador, Nicaragua, Uruguay, and Venezuela, where candidates proposing socialist-style reforms have managed to do extremely well and have taken power. It is obvious that socialism has a broader appeal in the developing world than in the European states, North America, or Japan, though a distinction must certainly be made between the sometimes very lofty ideals of socialisms (and the corruptions of it) in the past while we recognize, on the other hand, the hard realities of the need for a welfare state that provides for such necessities as health care, retirement security, disability support, minimum wages, labor and consumer protections, housing programs, and disaster relief.

It should be stated at the outset that Stiglitz considers himself a friend of free but also fair trade. He opposes artificial barriers established merely to inhibit economic relations; but he strives for a level field of competition, and he knows and states the inherent disadvantages faced by poor nations in negotiating their positions and, should it become necessary, in enforcing agreements and their rights under these. The parallels with his original thought and legacies are obvious. Understanding the various stances taken by Stiglitz on globalization issues should therefore be seen in most respects as a continuation of the study of information economics; his critiques of the international economy and his most original contribution are all of a large piece of work containing any variety of complementary components. This can be shown, to cite one example, in his rejection of Adam Smith and "invisible hand" economics as solutions for the less-developed countries. This is a rejection both pointed and effective because he knows and demonstrates that outworn "market solutions" are still being offered up by international agencies and by the governments of the rich countries decades after publication of his original research findings. Any basic homework on economics would reveal the narrow-mindedness and thoughtlessness of such approaches.[13]

What is globalization? The term certainly has a benign ring to it, and it can paint images in some minds of a world that is progressing, perhaps inevitably, towards greater understanding and mutual respect under the auspices and stewardship of international trade and the impacts this will bring about in such areas as education, people-to-people exchanges, tourism, expat living, and eventually a new dawn of peace, prosperity, and an essential but broadly-shared awareness of the planet's environmental needs. One sufficiently convinced of this benign image and the trends it sets in motion might even trace its origins back to institutions and initiatives like the United Nations and the League of Nations, the Hague Convention of 1899, or the Congress of Vienna of 1815, though these did not give economics a primary focus; even longer ago, if we choose, we can in some way surely relate globalization and some of its allure to the exploratory commerce and romantic adventures of Marco Polo. Stiglitz prefers a much more prescribed and precise definition which emphasizes, quite forcefully, the economic issues dominating this subject today. He believes that

> Fundamentally, it is the closer integration of the countries and the peoples of the world . . . brought about by the enormous reduction of costs of transportation and communication, and the breaking down of . . . barriers to the flows of goods, services, capital, knowledge and (to a lesser extent) people across borders. [It is] accompanied by the creation of new institutions that have joined with existing ones to work across borders.[14]

It is unfortunate, Stiglitz would quickly add in any of the discussion of the basics of this topic, that the more or less successful assault against trade barriers (though these remain in such cases as agricultural commodities) is a development that has clearly failed to give us a world of fairness; quite the opposite. The advanced economies of the world and their institutions, whether we are talking about governments or the profit-seekers of the multinational corporate entities, hold nearly all of the advantages in any bargaining or trade agreements. Simultaneously, their supporters—or what we might frankly call sponsors or affiliates—in the World Bank, the International Monetary Fund, and the World Trade Organization, as well as a number of other lending institutions and aid donor organizations, such as the Asian Development Bank, have created an atmosphere in which poor nations are offered few or no choices concerning their development futures. This dominance even extends to the United Nations and many of its agencies and decision-making bodies, and it is found as well within the leadership and influential forces directing the fates of many countries. The Washington Consensus holds a dominant position on all matters of trade, aid, and development, always supplying ideological answers for the world's economic and political problems, answers that are invariably and consistently within the frameworks of market solutions. These coincide neatly with the aims and interests of the multinational corporations, but they do not include advice or input from organizations focused upon peasant interests, labor concerns, environmental issues, or even the often-well-informed NGOs familiar with globalization issues and with the countries affected by them. Diplomats, trade representatives, and other officials and activists involved directly with these issues also have an instantaneous ability to identify the "good guys" and movements on the world stage (the United States and the West, and the states and groups usually supporting them) as well as the pariahs (Venezuela and its Latin American allies, any number of Arab states, and certainly Iran.)[15] Stiglitz believes that America's self-interest must be defined quite differently, and that the Washington Consensus cannot appreciate nor even calculate the long-term consequences. He insists that globalization has become associated with growing inequalities, and unless policies are put into place to counter these, there can be increasing political and social instability.

MILITARY POWER AND THE WORLD ECONOMY

Military power plays a role in all this. It provides a background undoubtedly influencing decision-making in the economic arena, since military and economic powers are mutually supportive and reinforcing. The advanced economies hold a near-monopoly in terms of weaponry, both nuclear and conventional, and in most cases, can field an army of significant size. The planet's leader in this category is of course the United States, which has more armed might than the rest of the world combined. (The expense and waste involved in Pentagon spending, many or most observers say, truly staggers the imagination.) It is officially claimed that the U. S. has more than five hundred bases scattered around the world, though the actual number is more likely within the range of 800–1,100.[16] The years since 2001 have seen the U. S. depicted, in any and every country, as a unilateral policy-maker that prefers to carry out preemptive, first-strike scenarios aimed at regime change without regard to the deaths and damage suffered by the population. Certainly the BBC and Al-Jazeera English, though their emphases and reportage contrast considerably, often appear to hold this view. It remains true—at least we can hope it is true—that the U. S. and the other wealthy nations are in most cases unlikely to resort to military solutions to enforce their economic prerogatives; but this kind of power is always respected and, in its own way, is also an economic wedge as well as a source of prestige within the international community. And this factor by itself can provide an influence of great moment since all of the actors in the world arena know that globalization is not merely an economic phenomenon; it is an arena of security issues as well. There is even an argument made, perhaps with increasing force, that says it is really too bad that the United States now enjoys the prerogatives of a unipolar system because this means that all nations must depend, in some measure or another, upon the power, judgment, stability, and sheer capabilities of the Americans; and that the supposed exercise of these in the past decade or so has failed miserably on all fronts.[17] Whatever the case may be, it must be borne in mind that the Washington Consensus, an invention of the neo-conservative school of power politics, participates in the economic sphere in a way that is well entwined with the Consensus view of security and foreign policy issues.

There is an obvious interface of military and economic considerations within the "Third World" as well. Recognizing that the world does not really run on separate tracks is explicit and on view in the security concerns and discussions which take place at the many international meetings devoted to trade, aid, development, and the plight of the world's poor. The World Economic Forum, for example, includes security panels in the discussions it holds at Davos and other locations. The G-8 Meetings, which are organized primarily as a forum for the exchange of views on economic issues, are nearly always concentrated upon security matters as well. The interplay of economic and security issues is even more explicit and obvious at national decision-making levels. The Pentagon likes to sponsor training programs around the world. It believes that these will enhance military professionalism and administration in the developing countries, and there can be no doubt that some economic side effects are felt from this presence of the Department of Defense. Any number of African, Asian, and Latin American countries serve as hosts for training personnel from the U. S. Whether the goals of professionalism and more rationally-based administration are actually achieved is an open question to say the least. Authoritarian governments are likely to appreciate such programs very well, but we also know that they often employ their troops against their own people. In the case of Indonesia, which has an army amply fitting with its status as the fourth largest country in the world, my direct study and observation of this training phenomenon, carried out with the assistance and cooperation of its military, leaves many questions in the mind. This is particularly the case when the business practices—the Army there actually runs a wide variety of businesses within the country—and corruption practices are examined.[18] The U. S. military's program in Latin America, which was once called the "School for the Americas" and which resulted in death squads and terrorism scourging the poor in Guatemala, El Salvador and other countries, brings about an annual protest at its Fort Benning, Georgia headquarters. The overall record, though there may be some small benefit to this or that "Third World" economy, has an appearance and character which well warrant skepticism.

International political trends are unquestionably difficult to assess, but there is now solid evidence emerging that as some systems break down, particularly the Nuclear Non-Proliferation regime that has provided security for the U. S. and the world since the time of John F. Kennedy, the unipolar power dimensions that have enveloped the world since 1990 will be replaced by an unstable and certainly more dangerous era of arms races and potential chaos. As scenarios emerge, U. S. dominance in world economic affairs will decline in concert with any loss in military prowess.

ECONOMIC CONFLICT AND CLASS WARFARE

Stiglitz provides any number of conflict-based descriptions of the globalization phenomenon in addition to his criticisms of how these have worked in practice. The large and effective protests against the World Trade Organization during its 1999 Seattle meeting, he strongly believes, were the first tangible sign that matters had gone awry in the international trade arena.[19] He states that these demonstrations, and the many that have occurred in places like Davos, Chicago, and Manila, are evidence that many or most of the world's people think that injustices are brought about and facilitated by trade agreements or by the WTO, World Bank, and IMF, who often play an effective support role for these treaties by dictating absurd levels of belt-tightening to deal with inflationary pressures (often caused in the first place by the World Bank and the IMF), by smashing labor unions and peasant organizations through encouragement of such actions by governments, and by supporting corrupt corporations and privatization schemes while offering no workable solutions for the many problems of living standards, agriculture, debt relief, or the environment. The records of the IMF and World Bank in dealing with dictatorial and corrupt regimes is replete with horror stories in which these governments have involved themselves in the theft of lands and resources of their citizens, causing privation, disenfranchisement, and according to Stiglitz, starvation as well.[20] Any number of sources verify these charges, including the daily press, the International Labor Organization, perhaps the most conscience-guided UN agency, publications of the labor movements and many of the nongovernmental organizations of the world, and the *Multinational Monitor* and other magazines and websites.[21]

Stiglitz and a host of scholars—Walden Bello, Noam Chomsky, William Greider, and Jeffrey Sachs are prominent examples—have documented injustices and corruption visited upon the world's poor as well as the problems that arise from ill conceived programs and projects, most especially the many "free enterprise" agendas that have caused, and continue to cause, human misery. The situation in cities, hamlets, and farm areas across the world can often be quite brutal to behold. But it can be researched by those who are interested: the villagers and farmers can be interviewed, and any number of journalists and scholars have shown us what we can expect and learn from such first-hand experiences. It is obviously important to know what life is like for the poor of the world; and in my own cases these experiences demonstrate the appropriate character of the analyses and prescriptions of Joseph Stiglitz.

RESEARCHING AND EXPERIENCING THE "THIRD WORLD" ON THE GROUND

One of my first face-to-face encounters with "Third World" poverty occurred as I surveyed the landscape around a seafood-processing plant in Indonesia. Talking to the people on the front walk, I found that this plant offered the equivalent of a daily $1.15 to its workers for a ten-hour shift worked on six days of the week. Later, when I asked them why they were standing in front of this place, they told me they were hoping that someone inside would be fired so that they could have one of these jobs.

It turned out that this was a rather typical industrial setup; the only exceptional factor, I would learn later, was that this plant was out in the open, where some of its practices and operations could potentially be exposed. This is not the norm. Finding plants in Indonesia or other poor nations is usually a hide-and-seek operation, and it is not difficult to guess why this is the case. Dubious and unsafe working conditions, child labor practices, mistreatment, and low rewards for workers can be uncovered if one is persistent. Saddest of all, perhaps, is the experience of reflecting upon why the workers in such establishments are envied by many people, which is assuredly the case. The lives of industrial workers, obviously, cannot be the whole story. Most people in the developing nations are peasants who rarely see cities or factories. I often wondered how they lived.

Pursuing the goals of knowledge and experience, I slept on the dirt floors of Javanese farm homes and shared meals with families over a fairly extended period of time. Sometimes a family member waited to eat because there are not enough dishes or plates for everyone to be dining together. Their food comes from their rice paddy, naturally, but they usually have small supplements from the banana, coconut, or taro trees on their land. Their cash income can be as low as twenty-five dollars a year, earned perhaps from the sale of coconut husks. They will talk openly of their problems after an atmosphere of trust is created (which can take a considerable period of time and even days), and their stories are heart-breaking. A company involved in mining or agriculture sometimes has appeared suddenly on the scene; water and air quality, never good, are adversely affected. Corrupt government officials sometimes seize lands and evict the owners without compensation. This appears to be less often the case in this democratic republic today, but under the recent thirty-two-year authoritarian regime of President Suharto, a general whose installation was carried out with the help of the CIA, it was common for resorts, golf courses, or quite often, a project of the President's family to be placed on some luckless farmer's property. The more fortunate local residents, I was routinely advised, got jobs in the hotels or golf resorts.

Without any prompting (and after at least a couple of days have passed), old timers talk about and remember when the Communist Party (PKI) was big and influential, and they pointedly praise it for looking after their needs then despite its now-illegal status. Younger people endorse Islamic youth groups and NGOs who have sometimes proved helpful. After some days of interviewing, one conclusion becomes obvious: few of these people seem to know, think about, or care about the United States or, for that matter, about the West. There are merchants in city and village markets, however, who have thought about us enough so that they refuse to sell their fruit, cloves, or other products to Westerners; one of these explained to me that Westerners ("orang barat") are not good people. Such entrepreneurs are a minority, to be sure, but they are a part of the anti-Western hostility that appears almost everywhere in the world today.[22] Trade issues may appear to have little relevance for people like these, but some kind of image of the world "out there" is fashioned from films or contacts with tourists or occasional word-of-mouth opinions and assessments.

In Pakistan I was hosted and was treated very well by a wealthy landowner. His sons were my escorts when I made my ways around the country and, of course, into the areas dominated by his wealth and influence. The peasants on his estates were involved in temperate-zone agriculture, but many of them had jobs in their landlord's dairy plant or in his factory, which produced warm and useful leather jackets. Children liked to gather around me, and I was ready with pens, a gift all "Third World" youngsters seem to prize. One of them asked me why I gave pens to girls; they do not go to school, he explained, and I later found out they would never have such an expectation. Young men able to gain a measure of education often sought political jobs or even elective office. They took their cues from the landlord, a local power figure with strong political connections. At election time he would cast about 2,300 votes, since that was the number of people living on his lands. There is no doubt that he was *the* local political boss; and, as the literature on bosses attests, he could also be counted upon to carry out some benign and helpful programs for the community, recognizing that these were essential to his own self-interest.

The problem of poverty is a tremendous and overwhelming challenge, but it is not the central concern of this country's policy-makers. Postponing problems may not appear to make sense, but this has been the kind of agenda agreed upon by the country's elites, the relevant decision-makers. The security problems of Pakistan, as the headlines tell us daily, are a momentous and terrible distraction from the country's economic goals. The relative safety of Lahore and Islamabad, where I carried out most of my visit, disappears in the hinterland and in the surroundings of cities like Peshawar and Quetta. Industrial development proceeds more slowly than in India, but it proceeds all the same. The stock market occasionally displays dynamic growth, though many explanations can be offered for this. A strong impression remains with me that the elites of the country are often and surprisingly pro-Western and even pro-American, which is probably not the case within the other strata of the society. Like all poor nations, Pakistan has a great number of people who offer no political opinions; they merely want to sell their chickens or get on with their lives. This does not help those of us who seek out political or economic insights of the people, but it is a slant that should be understood. It should not be considered evidence of apathy, however, for peasants around the world have shown us they can be aroused by the right issues and the opportune time and place for their expressions and interests to be heard. No country knows this better than Pakistan, where poverty can be counted as one of the factors, perhaps the chief one, for the presence and influence of the Taliban and Al Queida.

LAND REFORM, A KEY TO POLITICAL AND ECONOMIC POWER

As suggested by the foregoing, land reform could make a truly revolutionary difference in how life is lived in the poor countries. The bullying and corruption of the land grabs in Indonesia and many other less-developed nations highlight what is *the* all-important and central issue for these societies, so it is difficult to see any agenda for progress succeeding without land reform. Stiglitz believes that this is the key to rural prosperity in these countries, for he holds that land ownership equals power, and power is the most important equation, the central point of organization and activity, in the rural areas and villages of the world. Poor farmers, as the experiences of Indonesia and many other countries have repeatedly demonstrated, have a difficult time holding onto their land against the pressures of often-corrupt corporate and government usurpers. In a typical "Third World" rural area, poor farmers do not own land at all; they are tenants, and their rents are excessively high. It is estimated that a world standard applied to sharecroppers, whether they live in Brazil, Indonesia, Pakistan, the Philippines, or Zambia, is usually fifty percent or more of what they manage to grow.[23]

Land reform, however, has never received any hint of support from the IMF, the World Bank, the WTO, or the United States Government. It has been my experience that raising this topic, as I have often done, in State Department, USAID, or other government circles will usually bring mild or sometimes even harsh reprimands of one kind or another to land reform adherents, and these warnings are laced with words of admonition such as "unrealistic" or "impossible" or "obviously undesirable."

Praise, if any is offered, will more likely be expended for finance reform schemes, such as the micro-debt programs of Bangladesh and Indonesia, which have been well-publicized (comparatively speaking), and these have unquestionably performed a service; but such programs do not really touch the issue of power or its use in any direct fashion. Stiglitz supports these programs, as far as they go, because credit has been a continuous problem for the "Third World" rural poor. But land reform is always the goal of savvy leaders and activists in Africa, Asia, and Latin America if they really want to get serious about changing economic systems that have not served the general interest well. It is the foremost area of resistance from elites, whether these are rural or urban dwellers, and the cynics and naysayers are probably correct in assuming that, short of revolution, there will be no major shifts in ownership.

Stiglitz is both unconvinced and undaunted, believing not only in land reform but in employing a wide range of policies—guarantees for labor rights and environmental protections, including global warming measures; a decline and, eventually, a total abolition of subsidies for agriculture in the wealthy nations; forgiving sovereign debt and replacing it with suitable levels and mechanisms for aid; permitting poor countries to retire debt with their own currencies; a scaled-down emphasis upon patents and intellectual property rights (an issue he believes is largely misleading and ill-defined); the opening up of markets for generic drugs; trade concessions for locally-based industries and economies in the poor nations; institutional reforms wherever these are needed including, and perhaps especially, those applicable to the international organizations involved with trade agreements and issues; an avoidance of ideologically-based hindrances to development (as in the case of Article 11 of the NAFTA Agreement); and most certainly, a broad and specific encouragement for development in both the political and economic spheres of endeavor.[24]

All of these positions, including the latter, are controversial, sometimes markedly so, but Stiglitz makes cogent and well-reasoned arguments in each case. On the question of a level playing field, he points out that most of the world's population lives in an environment in which inequality is actually *growing*; and the hope for a better tomorrow is, for now at least, a vain one indeed.

THE "RACE TO THE BOTTOM"

When Stiglitz writes and talks about labor rights and competitive development issues, he is often referring to the "race to the bottom," the multinational corporate focus and goal for wage levels, worker protections, and environmental safeguards. For most American-based industries and businesses this "race" had been confined in the past to the domestic labor market, where the biggest threats to standards were found in the South, the mountain and plains states of the West, and a few other venues prone to anti-union activities, state and local tax "concessions" or giveaways like taxpayer-financed plant construction, and what can only be described as reactionary political and social atmospheres devoted to corporate profits at the expense of public services and public works. Today, as anyone who has brushed up against out-sourcing knows, the field has now become fully internationalized. In this atmosphere the American South and other industrially receptive locales are often no longer competitive. Bangladesh or Honduras can process textiles, for example, with labor costs that are substantially less than a tenth of the going hourly rate in South Carolina.

Another Nobel laureate, W. Arthur Lewis, predicted the inevitability of the "race to the bottom" in a well-known article published in 1954.[25] Lewis, who began life as a citizen of the "Third World," demonstrated with considerable prescience how labor and investment patterns work internationally. He set out a model of no particular complexity, though it can be seen from the date of his work that information economics and its findings were not available to him. His model derives two basic requirements for a nation to become the recipient of capital investment, whether such investment is domestically or internationally based. The first of these is wage levels, which reflect whether a surplus pool of labor exists, as it often does, that can be profitably exploited. The second requirement relates to nutrition levels. The work force must be sufficiently skilled and must have enough physical energy to put in a day's work in a factory, shop, or other work place. (Until very recently, Bangladesh, to cite one example, was unable to compete at all for industrial investment because of inadequate nutrition levels, and this problem still remains far from resolved.) My own research confirms the Lewis thesis; but in examining the economies of East Asia, for example, it proved necessary to add two other investment-related components—infrastructure (roads, education, power systems, and amenities for executives, for example) and political stability.[26] Lewis has been proved wrong in one of his judgments, namely that inequality is good for development and economic growth because the rich are the best source of capital accumulation and in vestment; the more recent researches of Stiglitz amply demonstrate that equality is the principle which best enhances growth.[27]

The most disruptive element of these four for the international economy is the first of these, wage levels. Any reading of *Globalization and Its Discontents* or other Stiglitz works will show that while he abhors artificial barriers and is a strong proponent of international trade, he does not favor decimation of an economy by competitive pressures, whether these emanate from a wealthier or from a less-developed economy, merely for the sake of such slogans as "free trade" or "free enterprise." He has repeatedly pointed out, and is supported by a diverse set of allies and sources, that access to markets, although assuredly a benefit for the less-developed nations, is hardly enough to lift their people out of poverty. Similar analyses are made and supported by Jeffrey Sachs, the International Labor Organization, the Union Network International, and the International Confederation of Free Trade Unions.

"TRADE, NOT AID"—THE CRY OF MANY DINOSAURS

Corporate industrial location strategies and trade advantages, often accompanied by employment ruptures and other severe economic dislocations, represent an ample set of problems; but we must also consider the contributions of certain bands of analysts and critics addressing the issues of aid and development. Many of these are associated with the shallow-level "studies" produced by the notorious and exploitative ideological foundations, which, sad to say, are still tax-exempt as of today and are therefore government-subsidized. Wage data, development glitches of one kind or another, or perhaps the trends set in motion by the international economy are seized upon by these cynical commentators. A plethora of tired and tiring examinations of aid and assistance, as well as criticisms of those who, like Stiglitz, argue for some sense of consideration of the interests of the poor of the world, have placed their emphases upon the problems of aid and development while giving correspondingly little attention to the success stories. A Center for Global Development study that has largely been ignored shows that foreign aid targeted at stimulating immediate economic growth, as opposed to dealing with sudden or imminent crises, has had a substantially beneficial effect everywhere it has been tried. And aid, as study after study corroborates, is correlative to economic growth.[28] Tragically, and doubly so in light of these findings, development has reached an administrative nadir in the United States. Ideological meddling by the executive branch has had corrosive effects not only upon USAID, but on Food for Peace as well and even the Peace Corps. William G. Moseley of Macalester College calls these trends "the demise of development."[29]

There are other attacks based upon ideological preferences for "free market economics" which threaten dire consequences for donor nations as well as donees. An irrational insistence upon a total absence of regulatory protections in any clime, a position some corporate executives would favor, is a sterile and at times pseudo-clinical approach for international economics. Such models have a neatness about them as they appear in microeconomics texts; but international trade is always a matter of great delicacy that can hardly be analyzed in terms of such models, however aesthetic their appearance. Obeisance to them is almost on a par with sloganeering one's way through the thickets of real world economic problems. Rejection of such nostrums is strongly recommended in the Stiglitz Nobel Speech and in his three books on globalization. A major part of the overall problem with international trade and aid issues is that it has become painfully obvious that few people understand them. There is a basic awareness that something is wrong, according to Stiglitz, but there is still a failure to realize that agreements like NAFTA (now known as FTAA, the Free Trade Association of the Americas), CAFTA (the Central American Free Trade Association), the changes made in recent years in the trading relationship with China, and certainly the establishment of the rule-making and -enforcing World Trade Organization, are accompanied by basic flaws. Among the greatest of these failings is a largely unwritten but well-recognized provision for mobility that is truly international and facilitative for corporations but not for people nor, for that matter, for labor organizations. Fair trade is no more than a utopian vision under these circumstances.

IMF AND WORLD BANK LOANS: DYNAMICS AND PROCEDURES

> [Globalization] has condemned people to death.
>
> —Joseph E. Stiglitz[30]

The descriptions employed by Stiglitz for the granting of loans and related administrative processes of the IMF and the World Bank are more acidic than in any topic he undertakes. In many or most respects he makes no distinction between these two most influential credit providers even though he may tend to focus, because of his career experience, on the Bank. He does not exclude the World Trade Organization from his litany of complaints about loan processes and their enforcement, either, because these three organizations are tied together by "triggers," a euphemism for an interlocking set of rules which signal, for all practical purposes, that an offense against any one of these bureaucracies is an affront to all of them. Signing up for a World Bank loan sets up a requirement that the debtor nation accepts every condition enforced by both the Bank and the IMF. These average 111 in number per recipient country. The two organizations operate with a set of rules that is actually more punitive than WTO standards.[31]

The history of Stiglitz and his tenure at the World Bank can be delineated by what appear to be three stages of activity. First, there was a low-profile period; none of the thirty-odd speeches he developed during his first year in office, which were posted on the Bank's website, were actually delivered. By late 1997, however, he was offering strident critiques of the IMF, most pointedly on its handling of the crises in East and Southeast Asia. The IMF reciprocated by asking the Bank President, James Wolfensohn, to issue a "gag order" on Stiglitz in 1998. But Stiglitz was not only undeterred; he extended his disapproving voice to the whole of the development policy establishment including, of course, the World Bank itself. He aimed his criticisms at the Washington Consensus, a view of international relations and economics he and others regard as reactionary and deeply opposed to the best interests of the poor nations of the world.[32]

A major document in the loan approval and administration procedures is what the World Bank calls its "Country Assistance Strategy." This strategy is set up for each of the poor nations, and its design is a unique fit of needs with the resources provided to fill these; but even though we are supposed to appreciate and accept this description, Stiglitz asserts that this claim is false. All of the strategies have been devised in a cookie-cutter fashion. They really do not vary from nation to nation. Each and every Country Assistance Strategy begins with the same four steps: (1) privatization, (2) capital market liberalization, (3) market-based pricing, and (4) finally, a "poverty reduction strategy," which is linked with a prescription for a system of "free trade" to be established.[33]

So, how do these steps actually work out? The first policy thrust, privatization, proves to be a total disaster. Privatization is, for the most part, an ideologically-based scheme with no tried-and-true record and no obvious benefits for the supposed beneficiaries, the poor people of the poor nations. Stiglitz likes to refer to it as "briberization." State-run industries, notably utilities, have to be sold off. Commonly, and some would say shockingly, a hefty commission is paid to finance ministers, and sometimes to other officials, for ridding their countries of these very evil publicly-owned corporations. The commission is a percentage of the amount shaved off the sale price of a national asset, and this shaving can amount to several billions. The bribe is placed, as one would expect, in a Swiss bank account for the official. Russia in the 1990s, according to Stiglitz, was a particularly painful case to observe; it had certainly been a totalitarian state before the Soviet collapse, but the people appear to have been penalized for bringing about change.

Parallel research efforts have developed conclusions that are very much the same. Their findings, while matching those of Stiglitz, provide some interesting subtleties and dimensions. Though the point may be obvious enough, for example, it has been found that American corporate interests that may not be attached in any way to the World Bank or the IMF have found it much to their advantage to monitor their activities, work with them, and reap benefits accordingly. In the aftermath of the Asian meltdown, for example, Jeff Garten, who had served as Clinton's first-term Undersecretary of Commerce, announced in 1998 that the countries of East Asia "are going through a dark and deep tunnel. . . . But on the other end there is going to be a significantly different Asia in which American firms have achieved a much deeper market penetration, a much deeper access."[34]

And by the end of that year, U. S.-based multinationals had bought a great many assets from Seoul to Bangkok at fire sale prices.[35]

The phase then taken up, known as "capital market liberalization," presumably allows investment capital to flow in and out of a country in response to the ebb and flow of economic conditions. But in Brazil, Indonesia, and other venues in Asia and Latin America, this period proved to be what Stiglitz calls a "hot money cycle." The investment in these cases flowed in only one direction—out of the country. It is true that cash may enter the country for purposes such as speculation in real estate or the currency, but this capital leaves at the first hint of trouble. In the atmosphere of a fever-driven outflow of resources, a nation's hard currency and precious metal reserves can be drained in a matter of days or even hours. In Indonesia's case in the late 1990's, the only way capital flows could be preserved was through the quick jacking-up of interest rates to super-high double-digit levels of thirty percent or even fifty percent or more. The draining of the national treasury, the speculative pressures, and the high interest rates caused the poor to pay a heavy price for necessities within this volatile and inflationary straitjacket. This means that the country is already being forced into the third phase, "market-based pricing," with its unfortunate and misleading connotations of acceptance by the masses of a deep, intense, and very sudden decline in their standard of living.[36] All of this is necessary, according to the Bank, in order to generalize the burdens of eventually bringing the economy back to a "normal" status at some future and largely unknown point in time.[37]

Stiglitz could have added that the serious crisis imposed upon Indonesia, which grew out of the Asian "melt-down" of 1997, quickly brought about a change in the government in 1998 after the people took to the streets to riot, burn property, and sometimes to kill and injure people. And he could have pointed out further that the corrupt military leader who was then the president, Suharto, relied for his economic advice on a celebrated group of vaunted "Friedman-trained" advocates of "free enterprise." These economists had mostly obtained their doctorates at Berkeley, which of course is not the university associated with Milton Friedman, but they had received and then had taken up his approaches to the discipline of economics and to the world.[38] The riots that took place in Indonesia, Brazil, Russia, Ecuador, and other countries could have been predicted, according to Stiglitz, because the suffering and privation of these peoples was intense and far too long-lasting in all of these cases.

"Free enterprise" means corruption, mismanagement, and riots when it is in the hands of the World Bank or the IMF. The latter required the Indonesian Government to end all food subsidies for the poor in 1998, deepening social misery and political chaos. The instability of Indonesia and other economies during this period, and its riots, turbulence, and even deaths, caused even further dislocations and capital outflows.

This great finance-churning operation moves finally to its "poverty reduction strategy," which is aimed less at poverty, according to Stiglitz, and more at enriching the Western banks and financial interests who have put money into the country and need to get it out safely. This operation has been planned *even though* a condition precedent for it is what the IMF terms "unrest," its description for what often seems to occur. The "IMF riot," a term Stiglitz chooses to describe this situation, is painfully predictable; it therefore follows that the way out of a tough situation for banks and other Western interests must be ready for implementation. Assets have been removed from the subject country to the extent possible, and during this fourth phase, which Stiglitz submits can hardly be viewed as "poverty reduction," he has found that these interests pick up new assets in the debtor nation—a mining operation here, a forest-cutting operation there, and other bargain-priced businesses; a fire sale of worthwhile assets, in other words, and this is an appropriate description in more than one way because these sales are often literally carried out after some fires have done their damage.[39]

The pattern that emerges from these stages of IMF and World Bank operations is clear. The real winners are the Western financial interests who usually, if not invariably, end up with a new set of assets that began to shift to these interests with the first orders for privatization.

THE ENVIRONMENT AND GLOBAL WARMING

On the environment and global warming, Stigliz favors a combination of measures that should mostly be seen as carrots, though a few sticks are thrown in as well: he favors sanctions against countries and industries demonstrating a lack of regard for ecological safety measures. He offers as an example a Thai shrimp farming threat to the continued existence of turtles; the WTO endorsed and enforced sanctions on this question. And though he favors U. S. support for, and participation in, the Kyoto Protocol, he regards this document as flawed in several respects. There are built-in problems not only of enforcement, but also with the failure to impose sanctions on some activities (steel production, for example, which he knows well from living in Gary) that are clearly harmful. Most importantly, he believes that an international global warming agreement should contain incentives for rainforest preservation, with environmental credits or cash being offered for such efforts to poor countries. The Kyoto agreement actually encourages cutting down these forests, the "lungs of the earth," because of its focus upon sanctions rather than upon encouraging environmental stewardship.[40] Rainforest preservation is complicated because of such variables as law enforcement, which is difficult to carry out in remote jungles, and the bribery and corruption which often accompany the cutting down of trees, but Stiglitz believes that a combination of environmental consciousness, economic incentives, and aid measures designed to help assure preservation could work very well.

Like most Americans, if polling measures are to be believed, he decries the Bush Administration's failure to cooperate with the international community on global warming and similar measures, and he condemns this government's chosen path of declining to acknowledge the scientific research and findings that are relevant to this issue. (President Bush recently acknowledged that a global warming problem exists, but he insists that there is no money available for combating it.) Another stimulus for the Kyoto Protocol is making an appearance now in the form of threatened tariff sanctions levied against U. S. exports (thin as these seem to be at times) in the name of fair competition. The French Prime Minister, Dominique de Villepin, who is promoting what he calls a "green tax," believes it is only fair that French and EU companies, who must abide by Kyoto greenhouse emissions standards, should compete on a playing field leveled by such a fee. He believes that their cost of doing business should be the same on this score as the costs facing American (or, more accurately, American-based) corporations.[41] This proposition, it must be admitted, could be complex in both administration and effects, but it could produce, at least in the long run, a reaction from the U. S., which has rejected the Protocol while continuing to produce more air pollution and greenhouse gasses than most nations. The Prime Minister is quite forcefully seeking to achieve one of the goals Stiglitz believes we should strive for—using the trading system to achieve social and political goals that will be fair and progressive in their impact. It is difficult to affect such mandates, to be sure, but insisting upon environmental safeguards may be the best place to start this process.

As the outlines of any number of global warming issues become increasingly clear, it can be seen that the wealthy countries, the producers of most of the greenhouse gasses, will unquestionably be in a better position than that poor countries in facing and dealing with the problems caused by climate change. The continent of Africa, which produces three percent of all carbon emissions, is in no way ready to deal with such challenges. Stiglitz has addressed some, though not all, of these concerns, but he will probably take up the remaining agenda in due time.

AGRICULTURAL SUBSIDIES AND EXPORTS

The longstanding tradition of agricultural subsidies carried out by many Western nations—the United States, Australia, South Africa and many European states—includes a former belief that told us that this was a progressive response to a major problem. Even city dwellers and suburbanites often support price support mechanisms, conservation measures, and programs offering cash payments to farmers because they believe that food supply security, environmental factors, and a sentimental attachment to the idea of the "family farm" merit their concerns. Realistically, the policies of countries such as the United States, France, and Australia have clearly shown that politicians and policy-makers believe that they must react positively to the demands of agriculture. These countries are ostensibly democracies, after all, and they are only responding to constituency demands.

Optimists may have taken heart with the Doha round of trade talks as they got under way in 2001. These were to be aimed, in considerable part, at reductions in agricultural subsidies, however these may be administered, in the relatively rich countries of the world. (It was with the completion of this Round—which many argue was never really finished since it ended in complete disarray—that the World Trade Organization (WTO) came into being.) The world is still waiting, all the same, for substantive progress to be made within this domain. The Europeans, it can be charged, did not respond in any significant way to this mandate; but neither did the Americans nor anyone else. Major farm legislation comes up for renewal in the United States in 2007, and no one in the new Democratic Congress anticipated or even discussed any changes that might benefit the "Third World" countries. The Bush Administration, for its part, does not appear to be even remotely concerned about such a policy direction.

Stiglitz and many economists concerned with international trade issues realize that the strong tendency within the developed nations to subsidize agricultural production—and to increase subsidy activity in response to any greater realized productive abilities of poor countries, even should the latter experience only limited success—will inevitably doom any hope for these disadvantaged peoples to break into international commodity markets. Round after round of trade negotiations have resulted in a continuing impasse characterized by rich-nation talk about the need for development in the "Third World" while the simultaneous thwarting of agricultural competition goes on. Although Stiglitz and other advocates of change for this arena speak out frequently, at times even addressing the forums where decisions (or, perhaps more often, non-decisions) are made, the responses have rarely gone beyond sympathetic rhetoric. In the meantime the crushing anticompetitive effects of subsidies continue to do untold damage, and the funding of these programs in the wealthier nations has now reached a level of more than $1 billion a day. It should be remembered by policy-makers and concerned citizens that agricultural products are in most cases the chief export items for poor nations; and if no progress can be made in enhancing their competitive position, then it follows that development aims and dreams must be postponed for the indefinite future. There is simply no worthwhile movement on this issue to date.

Somewhat remarkably, and Stiglitz points this out, liberalization of the services sector would yield even more benefits to the poor nations than would liberalization of either agriculture or manufacturing, even though all of these areas should be figured into a comprehensive reform of trade issues as soon as this is possible.[42]

The conditions facing these impoverished societies, however, cannot and should not wait any longer to be remedied. The West will eventually face more than mere grumbling. The WTO, the Organization for Economic Cooperation and Development (OECD), Asia Pacific Economic Cooperation (APEC), and various units of the United Nations, among others, can expect to see greater insistence and greater cogency of demands as time goes by. Embassy personnel can expect to see protests; and most importantly, the leaders of "Third World" governments are going to be under increasing pressure to respond to agricultural exports issues. They can be expected to employ as much leverage as they can to obtain an improved response on this life-and-death matter. And if they are imaginative and can work out various kinds of demands beyond the assumed issue of moral suasion—producing commodities deficits in one way or another, for example, or even perhaps causing currency disruptions or other financial problems, then the possibilities for exerting pressure are endless. For the moment, the people who are concerned appear to be waiting for movement on this issue.

It was interesting for me to find, quite by accident, that in two countries as widely separated as Indonesia and Pakistan, there is talk in their agricultural sectors of somehow and someday organizing a "rice sack march." This same term is used in both countries. This march would be aimed at the wealthy and mostly Western countries found to be in closest proximity to the homes of the marchers. To participate in this, according to ideas set out in both countries, a peasant would simply place a sack of rice on his/her back and *walk* to a rich country to demand a greater share of the world's largesse. This demand would be forceful because of the supposedly millions of marchers involved, and it would be difficult to ignore or manage such an expedition and assembly. Perhaps Egyptians, Sudanese, and Middle East peoples would converge upon Germany or Italy. South Africa would be an obvious candidate for visits from its many poor neighbors, and Latin Americans would of course proceed to the United States. All of this could be organized. Could it happen? Perhaps not; but the poor nations of the world appear to be increasingly responding, at least in certain respects, to many issues and concerns as though they are one large and unified economic entity. It would be in the best interests of the wealthy nations to never believe that the probability of something like a "rice sack march" is totally remote.

THE PROBLEM OF DEBT

The debt issue has been one of the paramount concerns of Stiglitz, going back to his time with the World Bank and beyond; and he and like-minded critics and observers have managed to make some notable progress on this issue. Any number of wealthier countries have indicated their support for cancelling the debts of the "Third World." Even President George W. Bush has made some gestures in this direction, although no one seems to have figured out just what he is saying; it all appears highly contingent at the moment, and in his case it is frankly quite unlikely.

The dynamics of the debt origination and administration processes, on the other hand, are not difficult to understand. Poor countries borrow in order to develop building projects like schools or roads or perhaps dredging to enhance port facilities, or they may believe they can improve public health in important or even dramatic ways. Lenders, representing international organizations such as the IMF, the World Bank, or perhaps the Asian Development Bank, manage to convince political leaders of the need to borrow. Commercial banks sometimes weigh in, advising the need for a credit rating even to the point of saying that governments should borrow just to prove their credit worthiness. And quite obviously, the current officeholders in the borrowing nations are willing to let their people see the results of increased spending for what are sometimes, but not invariably, good causes. It may be other politicians or civil servants who will have to face the music later, when repayments have become burdensome or even impossible to meet. For much of this process, however, Stiglitz holds the lenders responsible. They wine and dine their "customers" and provide what may sound like sage advice about their country's needs, ambitions, and future prospects.

Stiglitz believes that one category of these obligations, which he calls "odious debt," should be eliminated from this picture altogether. This is the kind of debt incurred by an authoritarian and undemocratic regime, which may use moneys for almost any purpose deemed important to its welfare. Pinochet of Chile undoubtedly used some debt proceeds for expansions of his army and police powers in such matters as surveillance. Suharto of Indonesia liked to build luxury hotels and golf courses, confiscating the lands involved at the expense of their peasant owners. Mobutu Sese-Seko of Zaire was probably the champion contractor of debt, just as he seemed to excel in pinching aid money for his Swiss account. Such debts as these, Stiglitz believes, should not require later-evolving democratic regimes to repay them. This is not only an unjust remedy for what is surely a dubious cause; but failing to pay odious debt could also provide an important kind of message to the lenders of the world, namely, that providing money for these kinds of regimes and projects can become a risky business providing no benefits for anyone except corrupt dictators.[43]

The results of what some people in the advanced countries may regard as profligate spending have invariably proved to be unpleasant indeed for the poor citizens of borrowing states. As much as seventy percent or more of a national budget can become dedicated to repaying debt, and this will unquestionably mean that the most elementary services in health, education, administration, and infrastructure maintenance—bridges, roads, sewers, or whatever—will be curtailed or postponed. Debt burdens are therefore an often impossible toll to extract from these already-poor citizens. It should be pointed out, in connection with this, that debt owed to private banks—most often the best-known names in commercial banking in the world—plays an important role in this scene as well. Debts sometimes originated from the public side of the ledger—from the IMF or World Bank or a regional bank, for example—are aimed at repayment of loans from these profit-making entities. It can be seen that all of this emits the odor of a shell game that can become complicated, bandying the poor country about within a debt circuitry brought into play from varied but certainly combined sources.

As unfortunate and mixed-up as such a mess implies, it remains the case that the risks for any of the lenders involved are minimal and sometimes nonexistent. Stiglitz's *Globalization and Its Discontents* demonstrates that, again and again, the World Bank made bad gambles; but the consequences for its officials were rarely of a kind that entailed much risk to themselves. In the case of private banks, there is often government insurance against losses on these deals or, if needed, even emergency bailouts can come into play to relieve these privileged institutions of any untoward cares. The response of Jeffrey Sachs to the problem of onerous and outstanding private bank loans to poor nations and the servicing of such debts is simple enough: don't pay them! Experience with this approach, which has been tried in Bolivia and other places, has proved that the country's credit problems, in the long run at least, were not traceably affected.[44]

Stiglitz proposes five remedies for the problem of international debt, and their essence shows that he has changes for the IMF prominently in mind. These are: first, do no harm. The IMF is so fearful of inflation and, to a lesser extent, of debt cancellation, that it ignores the need for economic growth and uses occasions of crisis, such as default or near-default, to lecture countries on their need (as always, or so it seems, with the IMF) for belt-tightening measures, controls over labor or peasant demands, and interest rate increases. One of the most devastating ongoing approaches of the IMF is to ignore completely the Keynesian findings that government indebtedness combined with lowered taxes and interest rates can often pull a nation out of recession. It insists upon an inversion of such helpful activity. Secondly, the lending agencies should not engage in counter-cyclical lending or, put another way, they should not demand repayment of loans at the very times during which the country most needs the capital. Third, there should be a reduction effected in the borrowing risks. There are many ways of slicing and dicing risk so that it can be parceled out over various areas and time periods. (Wall Street, Stiglitz points out, does this as a routine matter.) One way of doing this is to allow countries to borrow in their own currencies. Another is to extend insurance to interest rate and exchange rate changes; this would make the debt contracts more expensive, but Stiglitz believes that this may be a good thing if it discourages taking on questionable or onerous debt. The World Bank and other multilateral creditors could also strengthen borrowers by employing borrowing obligations in the debt markets of the debtor countries. An important consideration in this area of concern is for rich and Western nations to avoid exporting risk to the poor countries, a practice that is commonly carried out at present. The fourth recommendation is that countries should borrow conservatively, making sure as well that they borrow in their own currencies.

Borrowing, after all, often creates more problems than it is worth. The fifth and final point is that the international economy must have a way of planning for various contingencies. This common sense recognition should lead to creation of an internationally-recognized form of bankruptcy, which could afford needed relief to debtor countries. Such a wholly new arrangement must include various principles, such as allowing debtor countries to be relieved of enough of their obligation so that they will not readily fall into serious straits again. Stiglitz faults the United States for opposing and even blocking consideration of this measure.[45]

At the moment the international community appears to be far from any course of adopting such measures. This means that, for the time being, only a pessimistic assessment of the status of debtor nations is in order. The only foreseeable hope is based upon what appears to be an increased awareness of the overriding and burdensome significance of debt and its consequences. The debt issue is not so arcane that it escapes public attention or indignation. It is a subject of many a placard in recent years in locations as far apart as Brazil, Seattle, Davos, and Scotland. It is increasingly recognized that the one-size-fits-all approach (a Stiglitz term) to debt and economic development simply does not work.

Irony inevitably plays a role in economic affairs, and it is impossible to refrain from remarking upon the commonplace insistence of the World Bank and the IMF that this or that country should be repaying its debt because this is seen as an important matter of principle when at the same time the United States, the greatest influence and policy guide on these organizations, continues to rack up record levels of both budgetary and trade indebtedness (with one feeding the other to some extent), a practice that is so continuous and profligate that there is no end of it in sight. A better example could be set, even though the proportions and range often appear almost out of reach.

Remarkably, there are subsidies that should not be overlooked when the debt of poor countries is examined—subsidies paid by these countries to the developed and mostly Western nations. An intense set of pressures on these countries from the IMF, World Bank, and the WTO has caused (and in some cases has required) them to establish larger reserve accounts of currencies of the developed states of the world. In the recent past, the poor countries held reserves for perhaps three months, which on most occasions proved adequate though, on occasion, this was not the case. The worries about solvency and adequate debt repayments have caused these countries to increase these reserves to nine months or perhaps a year or even a longer term. This means, of course, that they must purchase more securities such as Treasury bills of the United States in order to strengthen these reserves. It also means, however, that T-bills and other developed nations' assets are subsidized through the mechanism of IMF-World Bank-WTO pressures. Three months of holdings should be adequate because these have proved to meet credit requirements in the vast majority of cases. It should be pointed out that Stiglitz, among many others, has advocated going eventually to a single world currency, but all agree that this solution is still far off.

PEOPLE ARE MORE IMPORTANT THAN PATENTS OR PROPERTY

A recent Oxfam International report contains the observation that people are more important than patents or property, a proposition that should hardly be controversial.[46] The topic at hand was the AIDS epidemic that has plagued Africa since 2001. Four million people on the continent have contracted the disease since then, but monopolistic drug companies control more than 74 percent of the anti-AIDS drugs and 77 percent of those infected go untreated. This drug company control assuredly does not account for all of the untreated cases, but it is a definite and overwhelmingly harmful factor. In the meantime the United States is increasingly forcing poor countries to sign trade agreements containing patent restrictions; and this means that the cost of drugs in Peru will increase by about 100 percent over the next ten years while Colombia and any number of nations will be required to substantially increase payments for pharmaceuticals. India, on the other hand, has been supplying the developing world with approximately two-thirds of its generic drugs, but the outlook is that this production will be severely cut if multinational pharmaceutical companies successfully challenge this production under existing world trade laws.[47]

These ultimately inhumane laws were at one time not possible, Stiglitz points out, but in the early 1990s the TRIP (Trade-Related International Property) Agreement was brought into being under the auspices of the WTO. Stiglitz believes that the negotiating position of the poor nations was absurdly weak as this Agreement took shape, in accordance with the findings establishing the economics of information. Any cursory glance at the dynamics and machinations of American politics tells us that drug companies win the day on nearly all occasions, whether the forum is Congress, the White House, or the Food and Drug Administration (FDA). The unusual Medicare Prescription Reform of 2003 reflected this strong-arm lobbying activity, both in terms of the legislation itself and in the dreadful and shameful process which brought it about. (A rules-breaking record time for a quorum call was set in the House as Floor Leader Tom DeLay and his henchmen secured a one-vote victory with a variety of carrots and sticks.) This giant backward step in health care inflicted a new emphasis upon privatization into the Medicare program and crated the now-infamous "doughnut hole," a period of years in which prescription benefits lapse altogether before resuming, an inelegant example of program design if ever there was one; social welfare experts often claim that this is the most unique and logic-defying provisions ever seen in a health care scheme. It also established set prices for drug products that the government, at all odds a strong negotiator, has no authority to negotiate prices and, voila! The taxpayers lose a bundle of money. Most importantly—and most damaging—this law further entrenched the drug industry, the insurance companies, and health maintenance organizations within the Medicare framework, where they had no presence at all until the mid-1990s and where their position can be justly regarded as a usurpation of the public's authority and wishes.

A similar problem has surfaced in the international arena, which should hardly surprise us. Stiglitz reports that "TRIPs imposed on the entire world the dominant intellectual property regime in the United States and Europe . . . [and this is] not good for the United States and the EU; but even more, I believe it is not in the interests of the developing countries."[48] The monopoly position afforded to Big Pharma has long-reaching and dire consequences for the "Third World." The Agreement essentially overlooks the real reason for innovation, which is to benefit the whole of society and not just a few special interests. The adoption of TRIPs, Stiglitz shows, coincides with a significant moderation in growth in innovation and the discovery of new medicines. Once again we see the failure of the "incentives" argument so often lodged by market addicts and apologists, and in this case the result is a tragic and massive loss of life.[49]

Intellectual property must be tailored to the needs of the poor of the world. Destroying lives for the sake of drug company profits is carrying "free enterprise" to an incredibly and severely damaging and inhumane extreme. New approaches to this issue must be developed as rapidly as possible because the results of inaction will be dire indeed. Stiglitz advocates (1) medicines delivered at cost to developing countries; and (2) the issuance of compulsory licenses by governments when the world is faced with a major health crisis. These can enable drug companies to produce an item and sell it competitively at a level just above cost, and this could be expected to have an effect in favor of efficient production of drugs in "Third World" generic labs and factories. The issue of generics is at the heart of this whole matter, of course, because drug companies jealously guard their patents. Finally, (3) Stiglitz advocates a range of measures affecting research and its findings while promoting availability of drugs. He wants the present system of U. S. drug research examined; currently the system is one in which the government finances research while the drug companies profit from this.

A second approach, which he does not endorse, would set up guarantees for large-scale purchases of drugs as they are developed and produced; but pledging such funds to the companies, most certainly, leaves their monopoly position untouched. A wiser path, he believes, is to set up an innovation fund directly encouraging a company to develop drugs specifically designed for the use and health problems of the less-developed countries.[50] Stiglitz could have added that access to various foods, some of which are essential to diets of poor countries, has also been denied to people in places like rural India.[51]

The life-saving drugs issue, perhaps more than any other, says Stiglitz, shows how multinational corporations have tried to reshape the international economy to their own needs. They have been willing to risk and sacrifice lives for the sake of profits, hardly a way to approach the world.[52] Such issues as this one, once they become generalized and understood, can reap yet another great whirlwind of hatred and disdain for the United States and the West. It can be said that Stiglitz demonstrates a peculiarly strong and courageous dissent in this area when it is remembered that there is probably no greater insistence within the opinionated structure of the Washington Consensus than its attachment to the economic and legal traditions found in patents and intellectual property.

There is a great range of issues and concerns surrounding agreements that provide protection for patents and intellectual property, far more than our space can manage. Though this array rarely achieves the importance of the provision of lifesaving drugs, there are, all the same, matters of considerable anxiety found within this range, including look-alike computers, book publishing, music, and technology that touches almost every sphere of our lives. Stiglitz takes a position on these matters which, in the main, provides little sympathy for what he holds, in this instance, is surely a monopolistic position of corporations in various services and industries. In this domain he comes very close to being at one with Adam Smith, whose most famous treatise was directed at monopolies and how to deal with them.

TRENDS

The euphoria of the 1990s, the early post-NAFTA period, has long since given way to a worldwide skepticism about trade agreements, multinational corporations and their allies in units such as the IMF, World Bank, and WTO, aid programs (which have always had difficulty winning support in the United States in any event), and any and all policies and institutions associated with globalization. Many people have suffered grievous harm in Argentina, Ecuador, Indonesia, Mozambique, Nigeria, the Philippines, Russia, Thailand, and a host of other countries as a direct result of international loan policies and trade agreements, multinational corporate greed, and the side effects of corruption and environmental degradation that have inevitably followed. The Washington Consensus, though it still has the upper hand, is challenged today as never before.

Intellectuals appear to take an increasingly negative view of globalization as well; any cursory review of journals such as *Foreign Affairs* or *Foreign Policy* (and any number of others) will show that though there may be no clear consensus on many of these issues, the critical and negative views are ascendant. These critiques, sometimes pointed and devastating, have helped in positing a more or less continuous theme and demand for reform and change. The world *does* seem to care, after all, about fair bargains and fair treatment, the environment, labor rights, human rights, political freedom, and what is sometimes an ill-defined economic freedom.

These many demands for change are unlikely, at least in the foreseeable future, to cause any of the institutions of the big movers and shakers to fold up or go away; but we have long since past the point at which these leaders and their organizations could remain comfortable, corrupt, insensitive, or satisfied in any way with the state of the international economy and its principal actors or programs. Moves are being made, in the meantime, to give NGOs a more decisive role in trade, aid, and loan processes, and labor unions are setting up meetings that cross international boundaries to set up strategies for dealing with Alcoa, for example, or with any number of other manufacturing, mining, timber, oil, and clothing firms. A set of processes are evolving which could alter the balance in order to benefit those who have not fared so well. Stiglitz and any number other experts and observers have noted these trends.

5

Challenging the International Economic Order and the Panaceas of Privatization and Deregulation

> How to fix the global economy [?]. . .Start with a responsible fiscal policy at home.
>
> —Stiglitz op-ed, *New York Times*, October 3, 2006

As with most keen observers, Stiglitz knows that the interdependence of the nations of the world, whether economic or political, mandates periodic examinations of the broad picture of both international and domestic interactions. This reference point is always at the front and center of his thought and writings, and it is particularly apt when the overwhelming influence of the United States in international affairs is taken into account. His experiences in government, whether we consider his work as an economic adviser to the Clinton Administration or as a chief economist at the World Bank, have also brought home this basic but manifestly important point.

Though Stiglitz was privileged, as a Clinton Administration insider, to observe at first hand some new and significant developments in international political economy and to offer advice on setting up new arrangements, he believes that

> Clearly, something was amiss in the way we were leading the world into the new international order. At the very least, we had not addressed the fundamental problems of instability. There was enormous talk of reforming the global financial architecture but not real action. Nor had we convinced many, probably most, in the developing countries . . . that [what] we were trying to create would work well for them.[1]

Complexity is the hallmark of international economic relations today, so this observation can be appreciated within such a context, but there is also gross failure here. Keeping up with the literature of international political economy requires both dedication and an understanding based upon multitasked and multileveled action and thought, and keeping up with the vast array of observers and opinions is daunting. Once the reading, writing, and thinking give way to any kind of pause or reflection, however, the conspicuous but perhaps most ignored fact in the world is that there is simply not enough being done to help the poor, according to Stiglitz, Jeffrey Sachs, Noam Chomsky, Walden Bello, and many others, including the ILO and an impressive array of NGOs.

PRIVATIZATION, IDEOLOGY, AND CORRUPTION

> . . . in some parts of the world, privatization has been relabeled "briberization."
>
> —Joseph E. Stiglitz, *Making Globalization Work*, p. 142

In America there is little question in this current climate that when a choice has to be made between public or private ownership, the public and certainly elite opinion prefer the latter. There are some signs that the public is growing wary of the inflated claims of the privatizers, but this point must still be conceded at the moment. Electricity, gas, nuclear, and other utilities are generally the province of privately-organized corporations even though this is not the case in much or even most of the world. Essential services such as airports, air traffic control, and even homeland security, as well as defense, prisons, and immigration programs are moving, or have already moved, towards privatization.

We all seem to know about the infamous deeds of Halliburton Corporation and its subsidiary in Iraq. The waste and other absurdities cropping out of this experiment will be investigated for years to come. A privately-serviced (and, often, privately-run) army is an absurdity on its face. The Brecht play, "Mother Courage," lampooned the idea of people making money from armies as they fought and died, which was the activity of the principal character, but this callousness could be dismissed because, after all, Brecht was depicting the Hundred Years' War. No one today would countenance such crass and selfish activity, would they? Well, yes they do; this is still the Reagan-Bush age, a time when conservatives and others support such schemes in knee-jerk and thoughtless ways. The services under contract are often not provided, whether we look at the provision of food or the critical supply of armor for uniforms and vehicles. There are so many hitches and glitches in privately-run wars that it would take at least a couple of volumes to recount even the most obvious cases before pausing to examine how we get out of this mess. A major hitch, which most of the 100,000 or more contractors involved in the Iraq war have learned well, is that the government cannot expect nor require a company to undertake its contract if conditions will not permit work to begin because of dangers or other roadblocks. The goal, then, is to get the contract signed. Never mind the company's obligations! These can wait for months or years; in the meantime, the money begins to flow to the company, and that is the point, isn't it?[2] Righting such wrongs has proved almost impossible; only Congress appears to be able to do anything about these shortfalls, and it has been slow to act. There is an almost insurmountable disconnect when private companies take over functions and duties that clearly should be left to the government.

Congress and the public occasionally wake up. Airport security, oddly enough, has experienced a reinstatement of public control because of the gross ineptitude of private contractors and the consequent public resentment. But immigration policy, the object of a torrent of complaints from every part of the public and every shade of the political spectrum, is administered by a private company that simply does not do its assigned tasks. This company was still awaiting its implementation of computerized operations in late 2006. The government could certainly have done a better job than this. But as this is written, the ill-fated hurricane relief efforts of the Federal Emergency Management Administration aimed at helping New Orleans and the Gulf region are being subcontracted to Halliburton apparently because failure in the Middle East merits reward in a different arena. Some of the FEMA money, however, will be politically siphoned into the Christian Right machinery of Reverend Pat Robertson for some of the relief tasks, though all of the relevant precedents show this to be an unconstitutional allocation of public resources.

Defense contractors could not survive without government largesse, favors, and understandings. (General Electric may be a major exception, but only because it is a true conglomerate.) Transportation systems are more of a mixed picture, with privately-administered airlines, railroads, and interstate bus systems existing alongside Amtrak and what is clearly a publicly-held majority of the metropolitan bus and rail systems. Public transport largely owes its existence to the inability of the private sector to find its administration profitable.[3] In another vital area, we are often told that we have the right to expect the U. S. Postal Service to compete well against UPS, FedEx, or whomever, despite any number of built-in disadvantages the law requires of it. The Postal Service is, all the same, run by a designated private company.

One of the most outrageous of all privatization schemes is one in which the Governor of Indiana, Mitch Daniels, and the Governor of Texas, Rick Perry, are currently moving to set up private administrations to carry out the mandates of the Federal Food Stamp program and a variety of related endeavors, such as nutrition and child care programs. This hardly makes sense from the standpoint of any conceivable public policy or efficiency arguments, and the whole scheme may well be illegal. Sally Mae's student loans, originally conceived as a helpful program for the furtherance of educational opportunities, have higher rates attached to them than when Sally was in the public domain. The evidence against privatization is hardly all anecdotal; the Economic Policy Institute has produced several studies underscoring these ideologically-induced crises. It is now estimated that the amount of privatized employment in the Federal Government exceeds the number of workers directly employed to carry out the tasks associated with services, policy-making, and administration.

Stiglitz believes, quite rightly, that America has gone overboard on the privatization issue. Both of his recent books decry what he sees as a continuous and unthinking preference for private institutions at the expense of public services, public goods, and public needs.[4] He sees this preference as purely ideological in nature, analogous to the automatic and ill-informed preference for "free enterprise" that appears to remain presently dominant (though presumably for a limited time now) despite its complete intellectual death. Stiglitz describes privatization of air controllers, for example, as an unexamined and largely unexplained phenomenon, but he has commented upon any number of other instances in which the faith practitioners continue to hold sway even in the face of mismanagement and corruptions of various sorts.

He saves his most bitter denunciations, however, for the IMF and the World Bank and their invariable insistence upon rapid privatization as a panacea for virtually every developing country. He also comments extensively upon the rapid approach taken—and insisted upon by the creditor agencies—in Russia and Eastern Europe in the early 1990s, and there is little question that this created great hardships and massive inequities that have persisted and have grown to the present day. The evolution of the Russian economy since 1990 has moved towards an ever-increasing concentration of a small number of very large firms whose positions, it is most accurate to report, have become monopolistic in their breadth and in their operations.[5]

The arguments for privatization are wrapped around many of the same assumptions Stiglitz has already destroyed in his major revision of our understanding of markets. These include talk of market responses to a climate of market enhancement and, of course, market efficiencies. It has not occurred to these ideologues that there may be any number of reasons why a Third World government has seen fit to set up, or perhaps nationalize, a given economic activity. Very often the reason is because no one in the private sphere had decided to make such an investment or commitment; and in such an atmosphere it is often quite unlikely that such an undertaking will occur anytime soon. It is not unusual in such environments for government to be the only supplier of capital available for an important but avowedly public purpose. In other cases there may have been a large-scale failure of a private capital venture that could not be supplanted by another enterprise because of a lack of interest or capital or because, by and large, a public entity is working out well enough. It is also the case, as one might suppose, that some governments do not take well to ideas of privatization. India, which is one such country, rejected Enron's bid to take over the functions of some of its utilities, a far-sighted choice if ever there was one. Russia and Eastern Europe, perhaps because of the conditioning of the Soviet period, seem to often prefer a public-ownership stance, and present-day Venezuela and its many Latin American allies seem all to be embarking, for good or ill, upon this path. These Latin Americans represent a rather large bloc of countries convinced, if the speeches of their leaders are any guide, that Socialism is the answer for their needs and problems. Asked about these countries and leaders like Hugo Chavez, Stiglitz explains their concerns within the context of the kinds of deals these nations have had to accept in the past for their oil and other resources. These were not fair; the prices forced upon them were less than one would expect under normal conditions. Chavez and the others have now managed to win better concessions, and the result appears to be good: " . . . these countries have put into place health and education policies that are already working, [reaching] the poor barrios for the first time . . . and these successes . . . account for the popular support of these governments."[6] Recent media announcements from Venezuela, Bolivia, and Ecuador state that these countries will be taking new routes on questions of government ownership and other alternatives to capitalist profit-making.

There may indeed be cases in which establishment of a privately-based service or function is the answer. Arriving at such a conclusion should be based, in all events, on thinking the problem through and doing the appropriate research rather than employing the knee-jerk ideology denounced by Stiglitz. Any assumption that privatization should be taken as a "given" is invalid simply because there is no research and certainly no hard data pointing to this as an inevitable or even desirable option. Different situations call for varieties of response; and a host of factors—availability of capital, values of a political culture, the lessons of experience, and certainly, efficiency and questions concerning the welfare of all parties involved—must be studied before any decision on privatization can be intelligently resolved. The literature on this subject is quite compelling in its overall demonstration that privatization works in different ways in different situations; and certainly the results can vary in terms of such matters as who benefits from it, who is hurt, and how income distribution in a given area or country is affected. (Reactions to any likely changes in income distribution, if these are to work against middle or lower-income groups, should always involve rejection of any such scheme on grounds of the public interest; this is shown below in the Fundamental Privatization Theorem.) It is clearly the case that the track record of privatization is less than compelling, and there is assuredly no science that tells us it is an obvious path to a better utility, transport system, or post office. There are many considerations and some substantial science, however, which work markedly against assumptions of privatization.[7]

PRIVATIZATION AND ECONOMIC THEORY

Stiglitz and some of his scholarly associates have worked long and hard on the issue of privatization, and their modeling and logic are presented in a variety of books and articles.[8] He and David Sappington put government privatization policies to the test in several different ways, but the Fundamental Privatization Theorem, their most significant contribution, was developed by asking whether a government could obtain more or less of any objectives it wanted through privatization of state enterprises. Their exhaustive work produced what Stiglitz terms a "striking result," namely that the conditions under which privatization could fully implement public objectives of equity and efficiency were extremely restrictive. The non-applicability of a privatization model, at least one centered on these purposes, was manifestly shown. Only in the rare instances in which conditions resembled Pareto-efficient competitive outcomes could there be any hope that privatization would work out for the sake of equity or efficiency.[9]

Many of the attributes of corporate behavior found in markets—risk-taking and innovation are notable examples—are unlikely to occur as a result of privatization; and social objectives, which can be counted upon to be one of the aims of government, are not merely a matter of doubt or conjecture; these are in fact unlikely to take place. Under ideal conditions the Sappington-Stiglitz Theorem on Privatization states that government will succeed in its goals better if it operates a service or industry itself rather than opting for privatization.[10] The real world can be quite different, of course, but the major point one should bear in mind is that there is no automatic nor decisive case for privatization in a given situation despite ideological insistence upon it by the political Right.

There has been an undeniable trend in the past two or three decades in favor of privatization in a variety of settings—the developing countries, Western Europe, Japan (which is seeking to privatize its Post Office banking system) and other Asian nations, and of course the United States, where the heavily-indebted, crisis-ridden and obviously incompetent Citibank is now carrying out the processing of passports even though there was no apparent problem with the former system. It should be pointed out that now there are problems galore. Estimates of the amount of privatization now found in the U. S. Government are not only pointing out that the number of privately-employed personnel working to carry out government services and functions has likely exceeded the number still employed directly by the government; they often include the further observation that the Bush Administration has carried out a virtual revolution in privatization, a response to its ideological bearings but also to its deep-seated and inveterate tendencies, now so well-documented and obvious, towards favoritism, corruption, and cronyism. This tendency certainly comports with the values and policies of the IMF and the World Bank, the very institutions Stiglitz has found so wanting in terms of rationality and sound choices.

The Stiglitz research reported here should be appreciated as a source that has helped to further the valid doubts about the efficacy and justice of privatization schemes; but it is also necessary to take the deficiencies of the private corporation into account when this issue is reviewed. The scandalous corruption and mismanagement of corporate businesses has been a perennial characteristic of the past three decades and, quite often, in previous eras, in industries and sectors as varied as banking, savings and loans, conglomerates, financial services, mutual funds, stock brokerage, electric utilities, defense contracting, insurance, mortgages, meat processing, food suppliers, retailers, drugs, chemicals, transportation, communications, household products, aircraft, auto parts, high tech, gaming, building profit, electrical appliances, corporate agriculture, tourism services, for-profit educational services, and of course telemarketing.

It seems clear, at this point in time, that many and perhaps most privatization schemes are not well thought out. Dispatches on the war in Iraq point the finger of blame at Halliburton and its subsidiaries over and over again for poor results in the supply of water and electricity for the people of the country. The prison administration record of the Corrections Corporation of America has been slammed by a variety of critics, some of whom cannot understand why there is any role for profit-making in such an environment. The government subsidies received by the many corporations feeding at their welfare trough also raise questions about whether it might be cheaper, or more efficient, or just an improvement in public policy for the government to carry out some activities that it now must contract for; at the very least, there would be no costs incurred for a net profit.

PRIVATIZATION AND THE WORLD

The answers provided for privatization questions by various societies around the world can tell us much, and the great variety of schemes and arrangements in existence should at least make us ask why only one ideology or systems approach should prevail. Germany, for example, appears at the moment to be on the brink of privatizing some of its programs and administration. The British, on the other hand, have become a wary and weary people after enduring the years of Thatcherite attacks on their National Health Service and the highly-touted, but apparently unnecessary, British Rail privatization. In the United States the case for government-sponsored and -administered health care is supported strongly by our experience with the services and hospitals of the Veterans Administration. Experts and professional judges of health care matters concede it is the best system around. Its clients have a direct input into issues involving services and provision of medicines and facilities, and they generally give an emphatic "thumbs up" to the VA. It beats private hospitals in quality of care for fifteen major ailments, as well as for technology use, patient satisfaction, and overall cost-efficiency. An important segment of veterans' care, the Walter Reed Army Hospital in suburban Washington, D. C., was contracted out to a Halliburton subsidiary by the George W. ("Support the Troops") Bush Administration. The company cut the staff from 300 to 100, and the subsequent scandal of neglect and mistreatment of veterans of Iraq and other wars provides a tale of tragedy and shame without parallel in the history of American government.[11]

Sweden, a stalwart proponent of democratic Socialism since the 1930s, has long considered itself the moderate or "middle way" between the private orientations of the U. S. and other Western countries on one hand and authoritarian state systems on the other. Stiglitz has taken a particular interest in its programs and administration, and has praised these within the context of their own terms and values without necessarily recommending this path to other societies. Some of his recent works, all the same, have stated that we can learn much from the experiences and approaches of the Scandinavians.[12] The most recent evidence of the functioning of their systems shows that they have quite successfully managed to come to terms with the challenge of competition from other countries, rich or poor, while retaining welfare state protections and high living standards for the populace. The actual amount of state ownership of industries, nevertheless, is a lower percentage than most observers would expect; but no privatization schemes appear to be on the agenda.[13] Even in the United States, the proposed privatization of Social Security and other social welfare programs (Medicare and Medicaid are often seen as candidates) has aroused a hostile response if the opinion polls are to be believed. The ideologues, ignoring these, strongly believe in the privatization cause. President George W. Bush's attempt is perhaps the best known, but President Ronald Reagan often spoke wistfully of the demise of Social Security, and the tendentious and still untaxed right-wing propaganda mills such as the Heritage Foundation, American Enterprise Institute, Hoover Institution, Hudson Institute, and Cato are always bringing it up, though never with a credible study supporting their claims. All of these and other elements of the Right have honed the flat-earth argument that Social Security is going broke even though it is quite obvious that a combination of normal-level productivity increases, long-range demographics, and having the rich folks join the system will keep it all quite solvent until sometime around 2090.[14] And speaking of flat things, the tax structure supporting Social Security could certainly be improved in major ways.

These conservative and extremist attacks, combined with the substantial damage corporations have carried out against employee pension programs and the shifting of ever-greater amounts of national income into the very upper reaches of the income brackets, have combined to create a public opinion majority believing that children of middle-income families will experience and suffer with living standards lower than those of their parents.[15]

It is fair to say that Stiglitz regards privatization as part of the same moldy cloth from which "free enterprise" was derived, and his writings betray an impatience and weariness with the issue. It is a cause and a platform that, most unfortunately, is more than just an academic debate topic. Recent experiences in the U. S. economy have shown that privatization often results in great losses of public input into policy and the economic process; in addition, people have had to pay for costly revisions of social and economic arrangements that previously were devoid of any need for "profitability," however this may be attained. Very serious cuts and losses of services they depend upon in areas like health care, emergency services, pensions, and education have all been damaged by these recent changes. The drug industry-oriented Medicare prescription legislation of 2004 is a clear example of this.

Stiglitz has imposed grave new weaknesses upon the arguments of privatization advocates with his convincing theoretical work and his discussions of the topic in his books, and he has also accomplished this further with his debunking of "free enterprise" and his general critique of corporations; but like many economists, he appears to let a great portion of the corporate critique fall to political scientists, journalists, and students of the law. He does not bother to point out, for example, that corporations exist by dint of privilege rather than by right, and he does not spend much space taking up questions of corporate governance or corporate law. A number of these and related concerns shall be addressed below.

PRIVATIZATION AND RESOURCE-RICH COUNTRIES

The world has any number of countries that fit within the less-developed category even though they possess an impressive array of resources. Their people are poor, but living standards can be expected to rise when these resources are properly evaluated and developed. It can be demonstrated that this was once the case in countries as diverse as Chile, Malaysia, Taiwan, and the United Arab Emirates; and no one could now reasonably argue that any of these should be listed among the poor countries. Able and honest stewardship of resources in nations like Brazil, Indonesia, and Nigeria could lead to higher living standards, better health, and improved futures for their citizens. (We cannot tell, of course, what the variable of global warming might bring.) Stiglitz believes that the most critical of the sets of privatization issues are found in these countries. Their potential wealth, to be derived from oil, forest products, agriculture, mining and other ventures has been targeted by the multinationals and is already being exploited by them while the IMF and World Bank, as well as other loan and aid sources, often perform their tasks with the welfare of these companies in mind. Stiglitz has documented this in his many and varied treatises on globalization, and he has performed this task while demonstrating the often fraudulent character of the privatization ruse.[16]

DEREGULATION

Deregulation Run Amok

—Title of Chapter 3 of Stiglitz's *The Roaring Nineties*

Deregulation has played an important and indeed central role in the international economy, especially in the politics of development. As far as the IMF, World Bank, AID and other players are concerned, it is one piece of a large scheme invariably sought and recommended. It precedes all of the other elements, in fact, so that the elimination of government intervention (often characterized as oppressive regulation) is planned with an expected set of tax deductions and anti-inflation measures before the last step is taken: the invitation to foreign investors to come into the country so that the citizens can eventually achieve prosperity. Stiglitz doubts the effectiveness of this scenario because overall testing and experience with this model have shown abysmally few good results. He holds that these plans have a shape and tone resembling colonial days, the times when it was assumed that the poor nations could never find their own way without Western assistance and leadership but were areas, nevertheless, that could provide dramatic economic gains for interests in Britain, France, the Netherlands, Belgium, Portugal, the United States, and other exploiters. The success stories of South Korea, Malaysia, Singapore, Taiwan, and earlier, of Japan, among many other cases, have demonstrated that there never was any particular need for this guidance.[17]

In the U. S. the demand for deregulation has reached manic dimensions. There is even an antiregulation journal called (naturally) *Regulation*; it is published by the dedicated "free enterprise" people of the Cato Institute, and such efforts hardly lead a lonely existence. As with the cause of privatization, there is a great deal of sloganeering, fueled by the belief of antiregulation advocates that their prescriptions need no real examination because theirs is a noble and market-efficient thrust that should be more or less accepted at face value. One can be sure, quite often, that zealots of this stripe have never heard of Stiglitz or of the economics of information.

But experience proves that they have stumbled badly. There is certainly no case of deregulation occurring in the U. S. that can or should be treated as an unalloyed blessing for the economy; and this is an understatement, for deregulation has usually resulted in disaster. Stiglitz has fastened upon one of the most egregious cases, the Telecommunications Act of 1996.[18] This law, and the trend it represents, has been a powerful weapon for undermining the public's longstanding ownership of the airwaves and the concomitant and wholesale abandonment of these rights and interests to media conglomerates. (The recently resigned FCC Chair, Michael Powell, and his successor, Kevin J. Martin, have used this legislation in justifying their diligent work for the cause of Big Media and its increased concentration.) The path towards this noxious state of affairs was first taken by the Reagan Administration with its abandonment of the "fairness doctrine," which opened the way for today's rightist-saturated talk radio and television. Repeal of the Act, a reinstatement of the doctrine, and a well-honed review of industry licensing arrangements must be high on the agenda of any future administration seeking an effective economic and governance structure, to say nothing of a return to the First Amendment and its protections of, and access to, advocacy.

In a different major area of concern, the extremists of the Federalist Society, among others, have called for the termination of the Securities and Exchange Commission, an interesting ostrich-like approach to the scores of calamities and corruptions displayed by the corporate world in recent years. Stiglitz, as one would expect, believes that the SEC has been far too lax about its job, especially on the matter of accounting practices and irregularities. The misleading work in this field, he believes, is traceable to the built-in conflict between the two major activities of accounting firms today, auditing and consulting, and the pressures of the latter upon the former. This played a major role in the Enron and WorldCom debacles, and it aided and abetted the electric utility pricing scandal which occurred in

California prior to the collapse of Enron. Accounting issues have developed within many other large business firms as well, causing inequities and injustices that have severely and badly affected various corporate stakeholders, including stockholders and employees. A major irony in this set of events, Stiglitz notes, is that they were occurring at the very time the United States was seeking to export its ideas about capitalism to the rest of the world.[19]

Deregulation of banking, implemented by repealing the Depression-era Glass-Steagall Act, is opening up a new can of worms. The built-in conflicts of duty caused by banks that dabbled in stock brokerage and insurance, and the resulting damage to the public, are the sensible rationale for the original passage of this Act, and there is substantially less reason today, amid the record levels of excess and corruption, to suppose that executives and officers can be trusted any more than they could have been in the 1930s. This point is underscored by the many legal slings with which the banking industry has been involved over the past two decades or so.[20] The accounting regulations and requirements of the much-maligned Sarbanes-Oxley Act perform a needed task of making up for some of these shortfalls, but certainly not all of them. And the dangers of miscreant activity in banking remain doubly threatening because of the many mergers and takeovers the industry continues to sponsor. This circumstance raises another regulatory issue, antitrust, but it is safe to say that this set of laws has been dead for many years. The most celebrated antitrust case of all time, the Standard Oil break-up of 1910, has now been undone; and though merger mania is not quite up to the feverish levels of the 1980s, when it spawned scandal after scandal during the coddling era of Reagan, it is as unhealthy for the body politic as it has ever been. Junk-bond financing, unregulated and unaccountable hedge fund activity, removal of mortgage administration from communities and then bundling these instruments for sale on the international market in dubious ways, dozens of types of tolerated conflicts of interest, and often-unwarranted downsizing are a few of the dimensions of this largely unregulated menace. Sometimes the only hope in dealing with the overall threat of this dubious commerce in recent years has been European regulatory activity, which has caused abandonment of some mega-mergers and a somewhat greater measure of control of finance activities.

Stiglitz is not only aware of the various direct foibles connected with deregulation; he has also demonstrated connections between this holy of holies and the stock market bubble of the 1990s, which was caused in part by the telecommunications policy disasters. He also recounts the various public miseries caused by the termination of airline regulation and, closest of all to his policy concerns, the varieties of deregulation embedded in the NAFTA and WTO treaties.[21]

Deregulation, he has concluded on many occasions, is cut from the same cloth as privatization and "free enterprise." On many occasions deregulation and privatization are packaged together in policy proposals, showing that these two types of demands are often viewed in the same benign light by their advocates. A recent example is an attack upon the National Park Service and its century-old legal mandate to take care of these precious parks. The political hacks in the Park Service and the Department of the Interior are proposing mining permits, more helicopter use, and more snowmobile and off-road vehicle uses for the park lands.[22] Financial benefits to be realized are the fruits of privatization, and it is quite a small number (as is usually the case) who will be enriched at the expense of virtually all Americans. Deregulation also plays its role since the abandonment of Interior's mandated care for the parks will obviously benefit the manufacturers and users of these deafening pieces of equipment.

Deregulation and privatization are matters that must be taken up thoughtfully, patiently, and Stiglitz warns, slowly as well. These are causes that have proved far too forgiving of the multinationals' untrustworthy conduct and excesses, even though they have never deserved the reverence and obeisance they receive from some quarters. But can Stiglitz and those of like mind stop, or even slow, this mania? For many of us, this seems doubtful at present or at any time in the near future, but politics and economics are ever-changing phenomena; the long-term outlook is that there will be significant victories against deregulation and privatization when education, socialization, media reform, public opinion and above all, a new set of political necessities are brought to bear upon these issues. And information economics will play a vital role in such developments while its alternative, ideological economics, faces a bleak future of irrelevance and uselessness.

INEQUITIES

In the dark period for economics, and for politics as well, that we can interpret as extending from the "fall" (essentially, the nonuse) of Keynes to the apparent and remarkable rise of information economics, major talking points about our economic lives centered upon the functioning of the system. The dominant media, much of academia, government, and of course the tax-evading right-wing foundations have devoted themselves to questions about how the stock market was doing, whether interest rates are too low or too high, the status of the housing market, what kind of tax cuts might be possible, what the transportation index and consumer sentiment measures were revealing, and, of course, trade questions. Ample time and space for right-wing ideology has been afforded within this vast array of presentations and conclusions, including blather about entitlement cuts, flat tax rates, incentives for this or that industry, the allegedly inappropriate and costly nature of environmental initiatives, a supposed need to get away from affirmative action and gender equality measures, and the ongoing assumption that the absence of labor unions in an economy is quite in keeping with modern needs. Attacks upon public education and the teaching profession have been virulent and have usually strayed far from the facts. "Class warfare" has become the chant when anyone has had the temerity to propose an increase in the minimum wage or perhaps stronger SEC or FCC regulation. All of these rude phenomena are ironic to say the least, since class warfare has been at the top of the agenda of the political Right throughout the last three decades of the century and the years since.

There have been notable silences on such matters as executive compensation, especially stock options, on Pentagon procurement procedures, on what "welfare reform" would really mean to the poor, on the energy costs of SUVs and suburbanization stretched to the far reaches of metro areas, and on the job growth claims of Wal-Mart as it has spread its cheap imported products and plastic nonunion stores across this defiled land.

More than thirty years have been wasted on discussions aimed at promoting even more economic inequality in the country than already exists. This lack of equitable aims, though usually muffled by ruses and various false claims surrounding these issues, have proved to be a built-in weakness for conservative activists' proposals, and this at least has had an effect of slowing some measures and actions even when they have eventually been adopted.

Information economics by its very nature is bound to address almost any and all questions of inequities. Its success within the realm of economic theory, though limited at present by broadscale ignorance, relies upon many factors, but certainly one of these is the inclusion of the interests of all in the definitions of economic concern and well-being thought to be integral to public debate and decision-making. This adds further potential strength to the new paradigm and portends great benefits for the bulk of humanity.

It should not be necessary to add that the term "theory" as used here is well within the context of the traditional scientific understanding of it. It refers to a system of conceptualization combined with factual data, which provide a useful yield of explanatory (and in this case, even some limited predictive) power. Theory in this sense can work its way through whole bundles of questions and answers and, in most cases, appears fully integrated and capable of being tested, in its whole form or in its particulars, for the truth or falseness of its claims. Information economics contains all of these characteristics and meets all of these criteria. Its origins were hypotheses, to be sure, but these have been tested over the years and useful findings have certainly been produced.

The reasons why it is necessary to state these obvious conclusions, sad to say, have a great deal to do with the strange age in which we live. Large masses of the American population, for example, will not even accept biological science, for the time being at least, if its theoretical underpinnings appear to be in conflict with their various superstitions or religions. Almost equally large numbers and their President cannot accept the overwhelming scientific evidence that tells us global warming and ozone depletion are threats to our continued existence as a species. It is quite obviously the case, in light of these and far too many other examples, that information economics may have a hard road ahead, though we should be able to assume—who can tell?—that this will be a short-run situation. Truth, after all, is difficult and costly to suppress.

SCIENCE TRUMPS IDEOLOGY, BUT IT CAN TAKE TIME

Anyone who appreciates Stiglitz's work can readily see that, in the long run at least, it shall triumph over its ideological foes. Science has a lasting quality once it is proved, and this cannot and should not be the case with ideology. Evolutionary theory has been given some challenges recently, for example, but all of these claims are based upon specious pseudoscience or matters of religious faith. No fair or even modestly acute intellectual observer of this controversy could assume that scientifically-derived formulations can be derailed by illusions, even if these happen to hold a segment of mass-based support. On occasion science can be overrun by better or more complete science, to be sure, as in the well-known case (to cite just one instance) of Newton and Einstein, and this has certainly been the case in economics. Kenneth Arrow and Gerard Debreu, as described in the first chapter, proved Adam Smith's work mathematically and specified the conditions under which it was true, building upon the work of the great Scottish philosopher; but Stiglitz and Greenwald later demonstrated the yawning gap in this information caused by the omission of information economics.[23]

It is unfortunately true that irrationally-based assertions or reactions to science can hold back progress for a time; history is replete with examples of this. In economics, one of the sorriest occurrences of this nature is illustrated by the great hoo-hah that accompanied a quite popular PBS television series on economics called *The Age of Uncertainty*, presented by Professor John Kenneth Galbraith in 1976. Galbraith's factual and quite objective series met with severe levels of criticism from conservatives, so that PBS, under pressure, agreed to have a conservative critic appear at the end of each program to tell us all, presumably, what was wrong with Galbraith's presentation. This was done in violation of the arrangements agreed upon for the series. But this insult to Galbraith and to the public's intelligence was not enough: PBS then produced a shlock series on economics featuring the ideological rightist Milton Friedman, who presented what was a combination of Adam Smith (as popularly perceived, not in the historically correct version set out above) with a heavy layer of monetarism and a resourceful but wholly eccentric explanation of what set off the Great Crash of 1929. (A badly-run bank in the New York City area failed, and this apparently set off a chain reaction.) But Galbraith's presentation, and his works generally, still stand and have borne the tests of time well, even though he predates information economics.[24] It was obvious that Galbraith's major sin was that of reminding us of one of capitalism's most dismal interludes, the Great Crash, and the excesses which led up to it.[25] Carefully coloring or covering up history has always been a major exercise, indeed a major goal, of a good many of the thinkers and think tanks associated with conservative economic causes.

Many other examples of irrationally-based derailment attempts could be set out here; but this cannot be our major concern. It is far more important to remember that science always and in all events trumps ideology. We can expect no more and no less in the case of information economics.

6

Multinational Corporations: The Major Movers in the World Economy

> . . . corporate interests have tried to shape globalization in ways which compromise more basic values. The fact that one area—intellectual property—has been linked with trade, but not others, like labor standards, says a lot about globalization as it is managed today.
>
> —Joseph E. Stiglitz, *Making Globalization Work*, p. 131

SOME CORPORATION BASICS (WHICH ARE NOT ALWAYS WELL UNDERSTOOD)

Multinational corporations are the movers and shakers of the international economy, and despite regulations, treaties, trade agreements, public opinion, critical nongovernmental organizations, and even occasional boycotts or strikes, they often (or even usually) appear to be virtually autonomous as their executives and boards make decisions affecting the environment, standards of living, working conditions, consumer interests, and a host of other considerations. It is therefore prudent to examine this corporate phenomenon, which is always taken as a "given" within the international economy even though it cannot always be fathomed or understood. The business press and other media seldom take it upon themselves to dissect this entity with any methods of care or precision, and this failure causes quite a large number of us to look to the economics of information and any thrusts it can or might make against the folkways, opacity and often-unwarranted secrecy of these often-privileged companies and their decision-making processes.

The term "corporation" can be traced to Roman times and the reign of Emperor Justinian. It is obviously related to "corpus," or body, even though we realize that a corporation is not really a person. The early history of the term and of this institution is sketchy, but we know that it was not used to define a profit-making entity in the common law countries until 1555.[1] Even after this date, corporations were organized, by and large, for religious, charitable, educational, and local government purposes, rather than for business or profit making.[2] Known at this time as joint stock companies, most of us know that they were decisively important in promoting the settlement of the American colonies as well as the exploration, commercial development, and notorious exploitation and colonialism imposed upon the East Indies and Asia and, somewhat later in time, Africa.

Their history demonstrates that corporations have invariably been a source of confusion and far too often of injustice as well, and this assuredly remains true today. They have never been popular institutions, and all countries and societies have greeted and treated them with suspicion if not with contempt. One of the more amusing incidents of corporate history occurred in 1250 when Pope Innocent IV stated that there could be no excommunication of a corporation even if it was convicted of a crime. His reasoning was that a corporation had no soul; it therefore could not lose it.[3] This heritage of suspicion and contempt is undoubtedly the principal factor underlying the dominant legal reasoning of the ages, still observed today, that an act of incorporation is not a right; it is merely a privilege. The legal definition of a corporation in the United States and many other countries is that it is an entity characterized by limited liability, perpetual life, and a persona. The persona is a fiction observed by the law for practical reasons (though the reasoning for this does not always hold up well), and the principle of perpetuity is based upon a similar and practical rationale. But it is limited liability which is most markedly regarded as a grant of discretion of broad legal and financial scope that is generally seen as the major reason for treatment of the process of incorporation as a privilege. This is no small point; one who ponders or encounters Exxon Mobil or Microsoft or Home Depot should keep this in mind when reading about these privileged entities or when delving into an annual report, which in few circumstances can be considered a fully informative document.

The legal theory upholding corporations and their existence, then, involves a claim that can be seen, as far as the law is concerned, to have a basis, a *raison d'etre,* that is similar to the one upon which your driver's license is grounded. It may be difficult for most of us to appreciate what a weak reed of authority this really is, since it is frequently and rightly perceived that corporations today are involved in a variety of great power games—usurpations and coups against governments in the "Third World," a host of undeserved victories over and against the public's rights to the airwaves in

America because of a history of outlandish regulation and lawmaking, the purchase of any number of Members of Congress, protection of crooked and overpaid executives, the undermining of labor unions and consumer rights on numerous occasions, and depredations carried out against our planet's environment. Corporations, because of these and other activities, have managed to maintain the atmosphere of mistrust and outright scorn that has dogged them through the centuries since their invention; and any casual reading of the business press (which, after all, is largely pro-corporate) or other sources will show this to be the undeniable case.

HISTORY OF CORPORATIONS

A thumbnail sketch of the history of corporations is necessary in order to understand how they have evolved as the world's most powerful private institutions. (Not all corporations are private, of course, and the term "private" seems in some ways inappropriate for organizations upon which so many stakeholders—consumers, investors, employees, and often governments—depend.) The most important periods for the evolving structure of corporations in the modern era are (1) from approximately 1720 until the late 1830s and 1840s; these latter years saw the requirement of individual charter legislation removed; (2) the go-go period from these years, including the dynamic growth of the post-Civil War decades, until about 1920, when the managerial class finally bloomed; (3) a period from 1920 until 1965 in which the corporations based in the United States thrived primarily upon a domestic market; this of course includes the very prosperous years of World War II and its aftermath; and finally, (4) the era of multinationals, beginning in the mid-1960s and continuing to the present.

Britain saw the enactment of the Bubble Act in 1720, a law seeking to end disreputable practices that had taken over the sale of company stock shares. Artificial bidding-up of prices, the spread of false tips and other misinformation, and a great variety of sleazy habits of stockjobbers gave rise to this law, which proved in the end to be only partially successful in controlling all of the chicanery. The U. S. eventually made similar efforts to control such practices, and these were legislated mainly at the state level; an intense period of stock promotion in the period of 1784–1791 resulted in an economic crash in 1792.[4] (There were other major factors behind this, such as failure of the currency and collapse of the U. S. National Bank.) Limited liability was not always granted in the charters authorized by state legislatures, and state-run corporations were commonly authorized to administer bridge tolls, roads, and other public ventures. A major revision of corporate law which took place at the end of this period was removal of the need for state legislatures to authorize each and every individual charter; a regulatory process was established for this purpose, with Delaware and Nevada proving today to be the chartering states of choice. The great anomaly arising from this period was the virtual absence of federal-level chartering (except for banking) in the United States, an idea supported still today by Ralph Nader and other corporate critics.

This issue is far from moot. Fifty systems of corporate law can produce any number of conflicts, confusions, and inefficiencies, as well as an ongoing and unseemly process in which the various states often see themselves as bidders in an auction devoted to offering the most tepid regulation. State domination of chartering explains the frequent use of Delaware courts as the decisive bodies in relatively earthshaking cases involving mergers and takeovers of what are in fact international entities. The economies and businesses of the world revolve around Dover! This also helps us to appreciate why South Dakota, with its host of anticonsumer laws, has become the center of the very profitable and usurious credit card industry. The monthly statements and our responses to them are governed, to a great extent, by the statutes of this lightly-populated home of great plains, dispossessed Native Americans, wheat farms, notorious antiunion laws, dead towns, and badlands.

Corporate charters were established as contracts by the U. S. Supreme Court in *Dartmouth College v. Woodward* (1819),[5] which held that state governments could not alter their terms, a general rule that is not invariably followed. This proved to be less of a barrier to corporate regulation, however, than a long-term infatuation of the courts with a doctrine of "substantive due process," which held that the Fifth Amendment's protections of due process and property rights generally forbade interference with corporate actions by Congress, the judiciary, or the states. This doctrine was not effectively brought down until the New Deal era, when the Court decided in a labor law case that other considerations, such as the right to organize unions and bargain collectively, were more important.[6]

The late nineteenth century was the era of the great "robber barons" and a time of tremendous growth in corporate power. The wealthiest families in America—the Rockefellers, Carnegies, Vanderbilts, and others—were closely tied to their companies and their great corporate empires. Their companies, along with a few others of note, achieved actual or virtual monopoly status in their industries, and there were long and difficult battles waged in the courts and Congress during this era and in the early twentieth century over the applicability of interstate commerce to their businesses as well as over the role of utilities, product safety, labor rights (essentially nonexistent until 1935), "substantive due process," the doctrine used to prevent regulation, and antitrust laws aimed at industrial concentration. Corporate propaganda surrounding ideological calls for the sanctity of "free enterprise" was undermined by magnates such as Cornelius Vanderbilt and Mark

Hanna, who decried competition as a threat that should be crushed, supported strong tariff laws, and often used illegal means to thwart their rivals.

Corporate historians tell us that by 1920 the ties between corporate giants and the founder-inventor families involved with them were loosened by the managerial revolution. The founder-inventor families were still enjoying the riches produced by their companies, but a hands-on approach (except for unique cases such as Henry Ford) had been largely abandoned. Though hailed in the literature of corporate history as a significant change, this rise of professional managers probably meant little to the coal miners, assembly line workers, or railroad employees of the time, or even to the generally passive stockholders. And the power and privileges of corporations and their leaders in the early decades of the twentieth century, great as these were, pale in comparison with the global reach enabled by their transformation into multinational companies, an evolution that had largely taken place by 1965.

The multinational era has produced the often-sighted complaint that the modern version of an "American" corporation may involve a headquarters in New York or perhaps Houston, but its charter is from a government such as Bermuda or the Cayman Islands, and its factories are in China. This has produced cynicism and also fear in America because popular opinion does not support the tax evasion represented by this kind of charter nor, very likely, does it want to see production centered in China or other relatively cheap labor markets. This fear is grounded in the all-too-obvious outsourcing of jobs now carried out not only by manufacturing firms, but also high-tech and white-collar employers and even by entities such as state governments. There is now a new fear, reported notably in the business press and founded upon the belief that financial markets centered in the United States—the stock exchanges, banks, brokerage houses, and related firms—are now losing their edge. Foreign stock exchanges are enjoying larger increases in listings than is the case in New York, and some financial services see keen competition arising from Asia and other areas of the world. A dramatic single event underscored this trend recently when Citigroup was forced to take out a multibillion dollar loan from the United Arab Emirates at an interest rate of 11 percent. A few business gurus and Wall Street wags attribute all or most of this trend to the Sarbanes-Oxley accounting rules enacted in the wake of the Enron and WorldCom scandals, but revision or even elimination of these rules, which appear to be sorely needed, would be unlikely to stem this overall trend. A great deal of the anti-Sarbanes-Oxley analysis fits all too neatly with the ideological strands of deregulation, which means of course that it ultimately explains very little. Corporations and their allies have a great many ready-made—though not always well-researched—answers for many such questions.

The business press, and perhaps some individuals in the corporate boardrooms as well, can take some comfort from trends appearing abroad which show some aping of American corporate traditions. Executive salaries and bonuses in Europe and Japan, for example, which historically have been substantially smaller, are now growing exponentially and may soon catch up with those of the United States.

These entities, it must be understood, are products of their history, an evolution which has never been able to shake or ward off the suspicions, wary cynicism, and sharp disapproval of social critics, the general public, and remarkably often, even portions of the business world and the business press.

CORPORATIONS AND THE ECONOMICS OF INFORMATION

Corporations are the first institutions likely to come to mind when issues related to the economics of information are raised. Stiglitz believes that corporate governance is an issue both of economics and of a participatory process, of efficiency but also of equity.[7] It is too often the case that hopes of participation are dashed at stockholders' meetings, where an agenda is typically run from the top. Embarrassing questions about executive salaries and perks, cash flow, takeover issues, or environmental or labor policies are sidestepped far too often; in the worst cases, a questioner will find that his or her microphone has been turned off. Shares vote, not people, and the executives sitting on the platform usually have an ample amount of proxies to insure their reelection to leadership positions in the company. Many or even most annual meetings fall well short of the criteria we have come to associate with the economics of information, and no one even pretends that these processes resemble democracy in any way. One change is in the air, all the same: the ability of shareholders to nominate and perhaps even elect their own member of the board may soon become a reality because the SEC is considering rules that will ease the way for this to happen. One should not feel grateful towards the SEC or its Chair, Christopher Cox, for this, however, because the agency is doing this under the impetus of a federal appeals court decision.[8]

The lack of transparency found in corporate structures, though justified in a limited way when operations, strategies, or planning are to be deployed within a competitive milieu, can create problems for various legitimate stakeholders—employees, consumers, investors, and communities in which plants and other facilities are located—whose fates are tied to companies. The Clinton Administration was able to enact a measure providing for two months' notice of a plant closing so that employees and affected communities would have at least this small period of time to adjust their lives to stark new realities. This measure is a good example of a necessary remedy for the problem of information shortfall. Pension funds and other shareholders have long demanded more openness on matters of social and environmental policy, labor policy, and executive compensation.

Noneconomic factors must also be borne in mind when corporations and their operations are considered, and these can be as central to a company's goals as its profit-making activities. Well-focused research has shown us that executives and boards of directors often have goals related more directly to the place of a corporation within the country's decision-making structure, its political life, or their own eccentric or egocentric aims and games. The well-established corporations of America and the world have found their place within the realms of power and privilege, and maintaining this place and attendant considerations—many of which are non-economic—can even be the primary focus and goal.[9]

MULTINATIONAL OPERATIONS AND GOVERNANCE ISSUES

> The large private corporation fits oddly into democratic theory and vision. Indeed, it does not fit.
>
> —Charles E. Lindblom, concluding sentence in *Politics and Markets* (New York: Basic Books, 1977, p. 356)

One of the greatest information lacks facing corporate stakeholders and the general public today concerns the operations of multinationals abroad. Union Oil has allegedly assisted the tyrannical Burmese Government in carrying out unpaid but compulsory work programs akin to slavery and forced upon peasants, to cite a particularly heinous example, while Freeport Mining, a gold-excavating company, stands accused of working with the Indonesian Army in an incident resulting in the killing of two teachers; and various shoe and clothing companies have been singled out for their employment of child labor. This kind of information is difficult to track down. Factories in the "Third World" are often unmarked, and factory facilities, which may have out-of-the-way locations, are often shared by different firms operating plants during different hours of the day or different days of the week.

The regulatory environments found on the international plane of activities are often quite different and generally less restrictive for multinationals than those found within the United States or, certainly, within the European Union. There are national code requirements which still naturally obtain in the international sphere; for example, the U. S. has a statute forbidding bribery of officials in foreign countries. The EU, to cite a well-publicized example, has clearly ruled that the requirements for mergers and acquisitions found in the United States are less likely to receive a go-ahead signal in Europe; a General Electric-Honeywell merger was stopped there, ending hopes of merging these two companies in the United States as well.

Despite such regional and nationally-based restraints and the complications and manipulations that accompany chartering, finance, operations, and production location facilities, it remains clear that multinational corporations are extraordinarily powerful and often appear answerable to no one. There are no countervailing forces operating on anything resembling a similar international level of influence—no consumers' organizations, no labor unions, no environmental or human rights groups, and certainly none of the NGOs found in any nation. The protests that have occurred in Davos, Seattle or other places are undoubtedly seen as nuisance events and little more. The bargaining strength of companies considering location in a poor country is immense if not irresistible; and many multinationals, it is often pointed out, control more assets and have considerably larger fortunes than that of the countries with which they are often dealing.

This set of circumstances amounts to much more than a routine problem for the nations of the world. The very lives of their people are often at stake and too often at risk because of corporate actions or thoughtlessness. Stiglitz believes, and has pointed out on any number of occasions, that the range of corporate governance issues is as broad as it is daunting—tax-dodging, executive compensation, the environment, working conditions, intellectual property issues, allocations of natural resources, and the list goes on.

CORPORATIONS AND THE POWER EQUATION

Some of the most important corporate issues arise from the character of corporations themselves. Stiglitz has written in any number of places that the division of ownership and control inherent in corporate legal and economic arrangements must be regarded as a built-in source of both conflict and confusion. Perhaps the most important issue of any of these, however, is found when one compares the *relative* powers, abilities, and discretion afforded to the multinationals against those of the various groups and peoples they affect. Any comparison of this kind must be informed by the power and privilege of the large corporate entities of the world and must be ultimately based on the great variety of institutional mechanisms available to companies for working their will—politicians who operate almost exclusively at the national level, the accommodating bureaucracies found at this level but also in the IMF, World Bank, WTO, and other international bodies, and perhaps most significantly, the mindset of these politicians and bureaucrats and their inevitable focus upon the real or sometimes supposed financial gains that corporate giants may produce, the definite lack of institutional barriers, and—lest we forget—their propaganda processes, often laced with market euphoria and, of course, "free enterprise."[10] And as corporate histories and thousands of analyses indicate, all multinationals possess a highly centralized structure capable of providing decisions and action agendas on short notice within an atmosphere of few or no dissenting opinions.

Any potential countervailing forces, and these can only be considered potential at the moment, are faced with enormous tasks of organization, consensus-building, and public relations, as well as overcoming of legal hurdles of one kind or another. Environmental groups, for example, are invariably forced into a great variety of ad hoc and voluntary organizational structures which amount to little more than platforms for the presentation of dreams and hopes. Labor unions, faced with the momentum of the "rush to the bottom" and a clear lack of organizational structures and unity with which to fight against the excesses of the multinationals, must gamely strain their energy and resources for the cause of what can only be seen as a long-term strategy of working across boundaries to develop coherent and useful strategies against employers who may very well be using one nation or organization as a foil against another. What some observers may regard as quaint and archaic calls for "international worker solidarity" may still be the only real or viable undergirding for strategies ultimately based upon pragmatism.[11]

Environmental and labor groups, NGOs, cooperatives, peasant organizations, consumer groups and similar organizations necessarily work with crowded agendas and mandates. The corporate world, by contrast, feels quite certain about its goals and expects to encounter very few obstacles along the road to its achievements. This quite secure position contrasts mightily with that of their employees and other stakeholders, and for those interested in Stiglitz's views on the multinationals, a number of complementary studies delving into the quicksands (for some at least) of corporate life are both relevant and fascinating.

Multinationals now enjoy a new and unprecedented pinnacle of power and privilege. The roots of this power are found in a tawdry history made up of both legal and law-defying actions and strategies based on an "anything goes" approach to politics, economics, and society.[12] Labor, environmental, and citizen groups shall be called upon to engage this overwhelming power in the years to come; and unquestionably, in its own way, the economics of information can and will play a role as this conflict develops.

WORKPLACE PSYCHOLOGY: OFTEN DEBILITATING IN THE WORKPLACE AND FOR SOCIETY AT LARGE

Carole Pateman, a feminist writer and one of the better-known sociologists from Australia, has studied workplace experiences quite extensively. She notes, quite unremarkably, that the psychology of workplaces is informed, most importantly, by the governance structure of business corporations. This structure, we all realize, can be considered a dictatorship, an oligarchy, or in some rare instances, some other kind of non-consultative and often imperious authority. Pressures are automatically created by such structures for the employees, who must follow directions and orders from the hierarchy or face serious consequences, including the loss of their livelihood. They must abide these undemocratic arrangements, in most circumstances, for eight hours a day, five days a week, or perhaps even longer. It is obvious that in such a set-up there are far more people on the receiving end of these orders than are found in the higher echelons of the company from which the rules and orders originate. In the worst work environments found in Western societies, there are permissions required for such elementary needs as visiting the washroom, taking a break, or taking phone messages. Sadly, these authoritarian arrangements are accepted by many of the people at the bottom as "the way things are," or even as the way such matters should be settled.

These arrangements contain significant—and, for social critics like Pateman, devastating—meanings for the entire culture. According to her, giving over a major part of one's life to an authoritarian work environment in which values such as choice, participation, consultation, and most certainly, equality—in other words, democratic values—creates a set of tensions within almost every individual who works at the bottom or even middle range of these hierarchies. The argument against arrangements of democracy, participation, and equality within corporate structures, almost always, is built around the benefits of efficiency and the traditions of entrepreneurial and administrative practice. She asks whether these traditions can really be worthwhile when we look at the social effects of the vast majority of employment arrangements.

Pateman points out that, quite ironically, the same persons who are subjected to corporate authoritarian lives on a day-in and day-out basis are asked to vote in national and local elections to choose public officials in a democratic and egalitarian "one person, one vote" manner. Choice, participation, and democracy intrude, however briefly, into the lives of people, and it should not surprise us that there is a great deal about the political process that the public seems not to understand well. Democracy, the system tells us, is a good and useful model for decision-making. Then the typical employee is supposed to forget these values upon entering the workplace. The evidence is strong that many individuals do not adjust well to an environment in which they must accept one set of principles during their time on the job and another set in their free time. Unfortunately, the much greater time frame spent in a dictatorial environment, with its cynicism and lack of respect for democracy or equality, will probably dominate the psyches of most people. And the consequence is that a psychology embracing authoritarianism is much more abroad within society than most of us would care to admit.[13]

Many readers will say that all of this raises a point that cannot be resolved with any foreseeable solution, at least for the moment. That is true; but it is a necessary factor when we seek to assess the contributions and problems given to society by corporations. It is a very big minus on the ledger of any judging process drawn up by thinking people.

AUTHORITARIANISM AND INEQUALITY

The trends supporting workplace authoritarianism include an overall and long-term downside move in wage levels and benefit levels as well, and this has been combined with an atmosphere of job uncertainty which, because of outsourcing, has probably not been seen since the Great Depression of 1929–1933. The threat imposed by outsourcing has received great impetus from trade agreements such as FTAA, CAFTA, and the trade arrangements accorded to China. No amount of employee defenses—additional training or degrees, for example, or a good work record—can insure any consideration at all. Some employers may observe the law requiring a sixty-day notice before shutting down or moving, a consolation of fleeting consequence. Economies competing with the United States, such as those of Western Europe or Japan, offer considerably more employment security. It would be a good exercise for readers to acquaint themselves with the works of Barbara Ehrenreich, whose reportage has often been based upon the everyday work experiences she has found in various locations in America. In graphic form she depicts the plight of workers with descriptions illuminating exceedingly well the sad statistics of incomes, work routines, family and social pressures, and the monotonously insistent greed of corporations.[14] Ehrenreich explores in painful detail the struggles of two-income and even three-income families whose wage levels make it impossible for them to pay for day care services, transportation, a sandwich for the lunch hour, or even basic necessities such as food or heat for the home. For these people, the corporation is an employer but also, far too often, a tormenting and law-breaking oppressor.

What may be most remarkable about minimum-wage workers in America is the size of their tax bill. Social Security is a very flattened tax system in which wealthier people receive larger benefits for which they pay a much smaller percentage of their incomes. For the poor and middle-income people this is a matter of inequities; for the well-off, there is no escaping that this is an enrichment through subsidies. Many or most people also live in states with regressive sales tax systems, assessed with even food and prescription drug bills, as in Idaho, and this means that they are victims of even more unequal treatment. In states like Arizona and Idaho, which exempt sales taxes for purchases like golf club memberships or dog grooming or a host of other upper middle-income concerns (Idaho has eighty-four of these exemptions), a shift of incomes from poor to wealthy is even more obvious.

EMPLOYEES, CORPORATIONS, AND LABOR UNIONS

The laws regulating labor unions and their rights to organize and bargain collectively are also unfair, even though there is a clear international consensus of support for enforcing these basic freedoms. Unlike the privilege of corporate formation, the law recognizes organizing labor unions as a right, and this is the case whether we are referencing international law, supranational arrangements such as the European Union, or national systems of law including, of course, the United States. Even the WTO claims that its 1996 Singapore Protocol calls for protection of labor rights and standards.

This consensus cannot prevent abuses of these rights, however, and Stiglitz laments the violations of labor law which crop up in many places—child labor in India and Latin America, repression and even the killing of union activists in a variety of countries, sham organizations claiming fealty to labor union principles and standards in places like China, and illegal antiunion activities in the United States that often cause enforcement officials to look the other way.[15] The presumably democratic state of Indonesia has violated the spirit of its 1998 revolution by enacting a law giving employers full reign on workplace issues and the question of labor union organization, while Mexico and any number of Asian, African, and Latin American countries have suppressed free labor organizations. Publications of Amnesty International, Human Rights Watch, and the ILO document these travesties, which also receive good coverage in the *Multinational Monitor*.

The legal environment is a paramount consideration when labor rights are at stake. The United States, most unfortunately, is one of the principal violators of these rights. Its basic labor law, the 1935 Wagner Act, requires the Federal Government to be pro-union on organizing matters in its Preamble. The Act was amended in a major way in 1947, although its pro-labor mandate remains. The 1947 legislation, known as the Taft-Hartley Law, gave states the right to outlaw "union shop" contracts (those requiring all persons in a bargaining unit to be members) and made it easier for employers to resist organization through both legal and illegal means. Illegal activity such as intimidation, outlandish promises (or any promises at all) made before a union representation election is held, firings for union activity, and perhaps above all, a series of interminable delays of the election process, all work to the advantage of the employer. A union-busting industry has grown up around lawbreaking employers, attorneys (who violate their oath of fealty to the law by even writing books advocating lawbreaking), and labor relations consultants, the vast majority of whom work only for the employers' side.

The slow growth and even decline of labor union membership in the U. S. must be placed at the door of this regime of illegality, aided and abetted by state governments and the Bush-appointed National Labor Relations Board (NLRB) and its rulings and administration. Opinion polls show large majorities of workers favoring labor unions in their place of employment even though these organizations are today mostly absent from the work scene. Union-busting firms such as Wal-Mart and the foreign-brand automobile manufacturers have active programs aimed at avoiding these organizations. All of this has international implications, because the American labor movement has historically provided key leadership not only in the ILO and the International Confederation of Free Trade Unions (ICFTU), but has also assisted in organizing and establishing unions in a great variety of countries of the world. If American unions become sufficiently weak, this will be a minus factor for international labor solidarity.

A solution favored by American labor unions for initiating real growth and overcoming the patterns of illegality and repression is a proposed Employee Free Choice Act. This Act would do away with much of the delay in the collective bargaining election procedures by simply allowing a union bargaining unit to be certified should the labor organization prove able to obtain petition cards signed by a majority of workers in a shop, office, or factory. EFCA received majority support in a House of Representatives vote in the new Democratic Congress in 2007, but it was not able to overcome Senate procedures which had been denounced by the Republican side when that party held a majority the previous year; nor could this legislation prevail after an absolutely certain veto by President Bush.

The Employee Free Choice Act could very well fail even if it achieves passage, however, because it would be landing on the hard soil of decades-long American traditions of workplace intimidation, repression, and tyranny. The "labor relations consultants," lawyers, and judges—as well as an often-hostile NLRB—would still be waiting in the wings to pounce upon any union created by the EFCA. The most probable scenario is that unions would still be stymied by the long-set patterns of gross illegality. An alternative strategy must be found.

Such a strategy must reject the "contracting in" system defining labor union membership now in existence. There are obvious advantages for one side or the other in labor-management relations from "contracting in" or "contracting out" systems; but since the inequities of the past several decades have generally been perpetrated by the illegality-prone forces of management, a "contracting out" method of operation is probably the only way to aright the system and promote a more even-handed justice. And justice, it is hoped, is or should be the goal of any system. Britain has had experience with both of these approaches. After long years of a good environment enjoyed by its unions, Margaret Thatcher, the Tory Prime Minister, changed the law in order to place labor in a much-disadvantaged position. The best precedent in all of these matters, however, can be found in New Zealand, where the provisions of an old law set up the assumption that every shop, office, factory or other place of employment would have a union, at least initially, and that such a union would exist in every workplace until the employees decided, for whatever reason, to vote it out. A "contracting out" system, in other words, prevailed there. This is precisely what is needed in America now.

It will be objected by some that such a system would be undemocratic (as though workplaces or corporations are involved with democracy, an absurd premise). But a right to vote a union out of its jurisdiction would be present after the union has had sufficient time to prove itself. American law, in any event, has already provided, in its own unique way, for a result based upon employer law violations. An American appeals court has already ordered recognition and establishment of a union without an election in situations in which a continuous pattern of employer lawbreaking is present.[16] The old New Zealand law precisely fits into this philosophic and legal (and, as we can see, American-based) mold, and it works, most fittingly, with the mandate of the Wagner Act, which requires and calls upon the government to be pro-union.

This kind of labor law enactment contains the seeds of countervailing power, the most obvious need for the working classes of America and the world. An AFL-CIO (or conceivably other) labor federation of 140 million or more members can do a great deal more for the working people in America and the world than the present state of affairs will permit. The political effects of such a dynamic labor movement, needless to say, could be a wonder to behold. And it should be remembered, above all, that this can happen. Labor contract bargains for wages, hours, and working conditions would still be plagued by information shortfalls arising from the asymmetrical character implicit in such arrangements, but the new political atmosphere bound to arise from a "contracting out" law, as far as membership is concerned, would provide impressive aid in reaching agreements capable of meeting the demands of justice.

Multinational corporate control of labor rights, labor markets, and working conditions shall continue in the meantime; most assuredly, this will dominate the daily lives and the ultimate fates of many or most of the people of the world, whether they live in developed or poor countries, a sad reality to contemplate or accept. It behooves progressive thinkers and supporters to organize the millions of potential adherents for these changes. The numbers, at least in the long run, are probably with them, and not with the multinationals; for the dispossessed of the world are always a large majority.

This proposed basic reform of labor-management relations, in all events, is one of the best and most profound applications that can be made in light of the revolutionary findings of Stiglitz, Akerlof, and Spence, and it could be an essential part of the reshaping the world so desperately needs. It appears obvious that we must shake off and discard many of the folkways and assumptions of an old and often despotic world as we build a newer and more promising planet devoted to peace, justice, and humanity. Many of those who do not want to go this way will eventually get on board, for we are now in a new day and a new universe as the economics of information and the reason found in its science begin to take hold.

Conclusion: Accepting and Working Within the New Universe of Economics

Economic thought since 1776 has been jarred and newly awakened from time to time by thinkers who have posited innovative theoretical frameworks we are all obliged to accept if we are to make any connection with the activities of the "real world."

Adam Smith demonstrated the dysfunctional effects of monopoly capitalism in his lengthy treatise by exposing the suppositions and activities of the Hanseatic League. He also made an essentially moral but also economic case for steep progressive taxation systems in order to deal with what he called the "wastrel" ways of those benefitting from systems of concentrated wealth. These can be seen as lasting contributions. Through the years and along the way, however, misguided devotees have decided to emphasize only some parts of his thought while ignoring other parts clearly as vital to our understanding. Much of the cure for this syndrome could be remedied, most obviously, by simply reading Smith's text. In the worst cases, these misunderstandings and sometimes farcical behaviors have led to cultism of one kind or another. The sporting of Adam Smith neckties is one of the more harmless manifestations of this; the Objectivist cult founded by the late fiction writer Ayn Rand, however, amounts to one of the West's sillier tangents and wastes of time. The thesis left to us by this "father of capitalism" that has been so heralded and so misleading has of course been "free enterprise," the belief in markets and their perfect efficiencies which Stiglitz and information economics thinkers have now thoroughly debunked.

A major revision of Smith occurred in the 1930s with the auspicious arrival of John Maynard Keynes, a creative and careful theorist who showed us how to manage capitalism during difficult times. Through a combination of fiscal measures and interest rate manipulation, he held, we could work our way out of economic slowdowns. He was emphatic as well as prudent in advocating the proper measures to be taken when times improved, such as paying down the national debt and readjusting interest rates. Much of the world heeded his theory and applied his remedies, and the experience of the U. S. and other governments demonstrated both the worthiness and the satisfaction with results one could expect in employing the types of measures he advocated. And though it certainly proved to be the case that many policy-makers and politicians would prefer to ignore him (and sometimes even despise him), Keynes is still with us. Fiscal and monetary policies adopted around the world reflect the pervasive character of his contributions. The Federal Reserve System and (though perhaps not often enough) the U. S. Congress and Executive Branch employ his counsel on a frequent and sometimes day-to-day basis. And, as with Smith, there are offshoots of his thought which tend, quite unfortunately, to crop up from time to time. The "Laffer curve" people described above claim to be wedded to their own version of Keynesianism, though this is a dodgy assertion at best, and Richard Nixon claimed to be a Keynesian because he imposed wage and price controls; but in these and many other cases, the major points of Keynesian theory are missed. Finally, there are those who reject Keynes out of hand, even holding to such absurdities as that he represents a "road to serfdom" or other dire fates. These detractors have not held up well over the years (see Appendix D), but Keynes and his work remain, with minor revisions, largely in place. The new universe of economics will continue to utilize and certainly accept him.

Putting John Kenneth Galbraith into this Valhalla of great economic thinkers might provoke demurrals from some, particularly those on the political Right, but the late Harvard economics professor has given us some basic and original propositions to mull over and hopefully adopt. In the 1960s, he pointed out that public goods are as vital and perhaps even more necessary to us as those of the private sphere, and that our commitment to these had waned for a variety of reasons, most of them political. He took it upon himself to argue that what some people consider the boring topic of public works must be examined anew and strengthened with a resolve that could lead to a better society enjoying the fruits of better parks, roads, bridges, water, national forests, and power resources. He was well aware, needless to say, of the limits of privatization and deregulation, and perhaps most of all, of the rapacious thrusts aimed at the public's domains of timber, mineral, and agricultural resources.

The case can be made that Galbraith remains largely unheeded on this issue. He had been alarmed, at the time of his writing, by an overall showing of little concern by the Eisenhower Administration, which proved in the years since to be something like a symbolic thrust against the public's interest. The real damage to our heritage and our system of public works came with the inept and uncaring presidencies of people like Reagan and the Bushes. The Reagan era was symbolized by the pathetic piety of James Watt, his Secretary of the Interior, a stump-producer and friend of the polluters if there ever was one; the George W. Bush Administration has felt a compulsion to erase public ownership of nearly everything, even the Army, within the eight years of its power, seeking to destroy the national parks, forests, and seashores while privatizing vital services and functions. But Galbraith's support for the public domain, public works, and of course public service has stood the tests of time and experience and now, with the even more costly damage of the Reagan and two Bush administrations being felt, he appears to be both teacher and prophet on these concerns; and hopefully, his case will be given its due.

Galbraith also has to be given credit for trying to teach us about the needs of the "Third World" with lessons underscored by his years as Ambassador to India; for pointing out such elementary but unobserved facts as the need for incentives for poor and middle-income people as well as for the privileged; and above all, for dissecting and detailing the Great Crash of 1929 in order to show us, ultimately, how we might avoid the excesses and mistakes that can lead to such a catastrophe. And not the least of his contributions is a 1978 study demonstrating that political power and ego games are as important to corporations, or perhaps more important, than making a lot of money. Galbraith is probably the most underrated economist of them all.

The new century has brought us gratifying and needed recognition of information economics and of the honors won and deserved by George Akerlof, Michael Spence, Joseph Stiglitz, and Bruce Greenwald (see Appendices A and B), even though acceptance and understanding of the new paradigm has been slow and even grudging. A new universe of economics has been created, all the same, and the world will have to understand it and, yes, live with it.

It seems appropriate and even noble that Joseph Stiglitz has decided, for his part and role in all of this, to concentrate upon the developing nations and their problems and needs as he takes up applications of the economics of information. He does not neglect concerns such as global warming nor the many issues of the environment as he works at this chosen task. There is a practical side to his concerns as well, of course, for it is in the developing nations that we can find answers not only to the overwhelmingly perplexing problems of poverty, disease, and education, but perhaps also to the broad economic issues of trade, aid, privatization, deregulation, patents, and agricultural policy-making. There is even a security side to these concerns, for any failure to address "Third World" problems shall encounter the dissatisfactions and unrest of the vast majority of the world's peoples; and the results of such discontents have already arrived with marks of grim forebodings for all of us.

The changes in thought, language, and calculation wrought by information economics amount to a renaissance for public policy-making and the disciplines of social science since so much of our past understanding and effort now must be revised or junked. It would be wise for the world to take up this new paradigm and its applications as soon as possible. A revamping of economic policy-making is obviously called for, but there are broad and inevitable spillover factors brought by this renaissance that will affect administration, resource stewardship, security concerns, finance policy, international relations, and the day-to-day work of agriculture and commerce, among other concerns. Most importantly, the very process of policy-making in government, not to mention the private sphere, will be revolutionized. Adherence to the need for information and the remedies aimed at affecting and expediting its presence and its facilitation means that we are all concerned with what is, indeed, a giant-sized quest.

Political and economic discourse must be transposed into words, phrases and tempos able to accommodate the new universe. "Free enterprise" is a good place to start this process, since its eradication as a term will align us with the reality, demonstrated by the information economists, that it is a nonexistent phenomenon. Politicians and public officials can make such an adjustment in their vocabulary; they have had to do this in the past, after all, when (for example) women's rights were finally recognized and universalized to a considerable extent, or when racism no longer remained in vogue in Southern or other locations. These and other kinds of adjustments can underscore our dedication to, and understanding of, a new and eminently more humane economic science. Those who, for whatever reason, resist such changes in the name of "tradition" or some other unscientific or improbable cause will gradually see their influence wane as time and reason pass over them.

The problems and challenges of the new century require us to utilize every tool available for the furtherance of understanding and our common goals. The economics of information is one of the more dynamic and practical resources fulfilling this need.

Notes

CHAPTER 1

1. For a summary of the work of Akerlof, Spence, and Stiglitz, see the Nobel Prize committee's explanation, "Markets With Asymmetric Information," dated October 10, 2001, at www.nobelprize.org/economics/laureates/2001/eco.adv.pdf. Summaries of the careers of Akerlof, Spence, and Bruce Greenwald, an important collaborator of Stiglitz, can be found in Appendix B.

2. Joseph E. Stiglitz Prize Lecture, "Information and the Change in the Paradigm in Economics," Stockholm, December 8, 2001. An abbreviated version of this Lecture can be found in *Economics for an Imperfect World: Essays in Honor of Joseph E. Stiglitz*, Richard Arnott, Bruce Greenwald, Ravi Kanbur, and Barry Nalebuff (eds.), (Cambridge: MIT Press, 2003), 569–639. The Nobel Prize in Economics is formally known as the Bank of Sweden Prize in Economic Sciences. A brief history of this award and the minor controversies surrounding it are set out in Chapter 3.

3. Greg Palast (staff writer, London *Observer*) website, October 10, 2001.

4. Adam Smith, *An Inquiry in the Nature and Causes of the Wealth of Nations* (two volumes), (Chicago: University of Chicago Press Cannan Edition, 1976); Gerald L. Houseman, "The Use and Abuse of Adam Smith," *Challenge* 46 (May/June, 2003), 108–11; Peter Nolan, "Adam Smith and the Contradictions of the Free Market," *Challenge* 46 (May/June, 2003), 112–23.

5. Joseph E. Stiglitz, "There Is No Invisible Hand," *Guardian*, December 20, 2002.

6. "Externalities in Economics with Imperfect Information and Incomplete Markets," *Quarterly Journal of Economics* 101 (May, 1986), 229–64. The authors point out that markets fail so often that they are forced to conclude that their claimed efficiencies have been woefully over-dramatized.

7. "Markets With Asymmetric Information."

8. Stiglitz, "Monopoly, Non-Linear Pricing, and Imperfect Information: The Insurance Market," *Review of Economic Studies* 44 (1977), 407–30; Stiglitz, "Incentives

and Risk-Sharing in Share-Cropping," *Review of Economic Studies* 41 (1974), 219–55. Stiglitz has also shown that the controversial assertions of environmentalists make sense even in economic terms in "Growth with Exhaustible Natural Resources: Efficient and Optimal Growth Paths," *Review of Economic Studies* 41 (1974), 123–38.

9. Akerlof, "The Market for Lemons: Quality Uncertainty and the Market Mechanism," *Quarterly Journal of Economics* 84 (1970), 485–500.

10. Spence, *Market Signaling* (Cambridge: Harvard University Press, 1974).

11. Stiglitz, *Globalization and Its Discontents* (New York: W. W. Norton, 2003).

12. Sachs, *The End of Poverty: Economics Possibilities for Our Time* (New York: Penguin, 2005). There are any number of writers who have similar or sympathetic views on issues of economic development, including Waldon Bello, Ha-Joon Chang, Noam Chomsky, Richard Falk, Jeff Faux, Amartya K. Sen, and Vandana Shiva.

13. *International Herald Tribune*, August 31, 2005.

CHAPTER 2

1. Stiglitz, Prize Speech, December 8, 2001, 472.

2. "Pareto efficient" markets, conceptually, are those that not only enjoy the benefits of efficiency but represent the best of all possible worlds in light of such givens as resources, market mechanisms, education, and systems outputs and efficiencies.

3. *Economics in an Imperfect World: Essays in Honor of Joseph E. Stiglitz*, Richard Arnott et al. (eds.), (Cambridge: MIT Press, 2003), 4.

4. (New York: W. W. Norton, 2003).

5. Prize Speech, 474. Though there are many examples of the theology that says that markets inevitably clear, a common one is the argument that trade deficits, at least in the very long run, will be reversed because the countries suffering from these will see their currencies decline, causing them to be able to market their products at more competitive prices. At that point, presumably, their trading partners will begin running up deficits. The British politician Enoch Powell often made this argument in the 1950s to assure the public that his Conservative colleagues knew what they were doing while the trade deficits increased and the pound kept tumbling. While there most certainly is a microeconomic model that one can guardedly employ in order to study or describe this situation, "real world" experience suggests that it can be viewed as neither dependable nor reassuring.

6. Prize Speech, 474.

7. The "rational man" model found in many works, including textbooks, was most notably used by Adam Smith in the *Wealth of Nations* and in other books; it has been a steady and sturdy model of economic life, and another Nobel Prize winner, the late Milton Friedman, used it to great effect in his heralded *A Theory of the Consumption Function* (Princeton: Princeton University Press, 1957). A formidable difficulty arises in such efforts, however, when it is realized that the psychology of an individual cannot be compartmentalized in this way because it is doubtful whether anyone employs a thinking process that is so robotic; see Duncan K. Foley, *Adam's Folly: A Guide to Economic Theology* (Cambridge: Belknap/Harvard University Press, 2007).

8. Prize Speech, 474.

9. See Footnote 10. Grappling with the term "political economy" raises issues that everyone in this field must consider at some point or another; as good an attempt as any is made by Elisabeth R. Gerber, "What Is Political Economy?" *Political Economist* 11 (Fall, 2003), 1–5. An excellent stock-taking of the discipline of political economy is found in Darel E. Paul, "Teaching Political Economy in Political Science: A Review of International and Comparative Political Economy Syllabi," *Perspectives on Politics* 4 (December, 2006), 729–34. This article confirms that Stiglitz's works and information economics are commonly incorporated into IPE and CPE courses.

10. The Bibliography and appendices of this book can provide further information and source leads. Political economy, it should be noted, is now beginning to incorporate findings from biological science in order to seek answers to any number of fundamental questions about political and economic behavior. This new momentum, now being developed in subfields such as voting behavior and sociopolitical attitude formation, holds great promise for the future of social science. For some recent applications of such formulae, see John R. Alford and John R. Hibbing, "Biology and Rational Choice," *Political Economist* 7 (Fall, 2005), 1, 3, 5, 7, 9, and John Orbell, "Science, Anti-Science, and Rational Choice," *Political Economist* 7 (Fall, 2005), 1, 4, 6, 8. This kind of research quite obviously adds a dimension of accomplishment, further expectations, and excitement to the discipline. On the important question of what boundaries and concerns should be central to the study of international political economy, there is a notable lack of consensus. As a field of study it attracts social scientists of many kinds, and historians have also made their contributions; see Gregory W. White, "International Political Economy and the Persistent Scare Quotes Around 'Development,'" *Perspectives on Politics* 5 (March, 2007), 105–13.

11. His association with the Clinton Administration apparently did not impinge upon his objectivity; his recent *The Roaring Nineties: A History of the World's Most Prosperous Decade* (New York: W. W. Norton, 2003), is critical of Clinton policies and approaches on many points.

12. *The Roaring Nineties*, 328–29.

CHAPTER 3

1. Prize Speech, 472.

2. Associated Press Report, January 8, 2007.

3. Joseph E. Stiglitz, *Making Globalization Work* (New York: W. W. Norton, 2006), 137, 275.

4. *Spokesman-Review* (Spokane), December 23, 2006. An interesting discussion of how poor, middle-income and especially immigrant persons in America face *disincentives* and added costs for their lives and their hopes for the future is set out in Jonathan Rowe, "The Freedom Tax," *Washington Monthly* (October, 2004), 13–15. Working hard and playing by the rules are increasingly seen as unworkable alternatives for many Americans.

5. (New York: Penguin, 2004).

6. Column by Andrew Serwer, April 4, 2005, 47.

7. A similar case in point is the Energy Bill of 2005, a long-sought measure of the Bush Administration; this costly tax depreciation give-away for the oil companies will fail to achieve any of its vaunted goals of energy conservation or independence. Exxon Mobil, the largest U. S.-based energy company, stated long ago that it has no interest in drilling and that it has a real problem of figuring out what to do with the $45 billion in cash it is sitting upon. Dennis Hastert, then Speaker of the House, gave an interview to MSNBC on this bill on July 29, 2005, and in what could only be termed a short interview, he used the term "incentive" twice. He has never been known to apply this term to non-elite causes or interests.

8. Galbraith, *The Liberal Hour* (Boston: Houghton Mifflin, 1960), 76.

9. Prize Speech, 476.

10. Prize Speech, 485.

11. Prize Speech, 482–84.

12. *Globalization and Its Discontents*, 94–113. Though market apologists argue that distribution of wealth is not a question that can address the functioning of the system, they will usually (if not invariably) become agitated, in any discussion of any moment, by assertions or proposals bearing upon egalitarianism in economic terms.

13. Many sources describe and verify these events; see for example Gerald L. Houseman, *Researching Indonesia: A Guide to Political Analysis* (Lewiston, NY: Mellen Press, 2004), Chapter 2, esp. 62–74.

14. *Jakarta Post*, September 16, 2003.

15. *Globalization and Its Discontents*, 89–132, 235–36, 255; *Making Globalization Work*, 34–35, 229–31, 243, 248, 261.

16. Naomi Klein uses the term "shock doctrine" to describe the zealous and greedy takeover of areas and economies in the wake of tragic natural events like the Indian Ocean tsunami of 2005 and the Katrina hurricane on the U. S. Gulf Coast, but also as a definition of these activities in the wake of fascistic takeovers such as the one engineered by General Augusto Pinochet in Chile in 1973. She believes that "free enterprise," in the final analysis, is nonexistent, but it can and does take on an expedient form that is a servant of totalitarian forces in the world, aided and abetted by people like the late Milton Friedman and the "Chicago school" of laissez-faire economics; Klein, *The Shock Doctrine: The Rise of Disaster Capitalism* (New York: Metropolitan, 2007). Stiglitz gives Klein a favorable review in the *New York Times Book Review* of September 30, 2007, 12. On "shock therapy" in his own books, see *Making Globalization Work*, 242; *Globalization and Its Discontents*, Chapter 5; and Joseph E. Stiglitz, *Whither Socialism?* (Cambridge: MIT Press, 1996), 192–94.

17. *New York Times*, April 3, 2000.

18. Justin Hibbard and Adrienne Carter, "Another Fishy Hedge Fund," *Business Week*, October 24, 2005, 36–39. This article points out that at this time there were 8,219 hedge funds administering $1 trillion in assets.

19. *New York Times*, October 1 and 2, 1999.

20. Stiglitz seems to prefer, for whatever reason, to analyze the savings-and-loan scandals of the Reagan years in making the case for the economics of information, and this is certainly a relevant set of incidents; Joseph E. Stiglitz and Bruce Green-

wald, *Towards a New Paradigm in Monetary Economics* (New York: Cambridge University Press, 2003), 277–79.

21. Henry Blodgett, "Why Hedge Funds Keep Imploding," *This Week*, October 9, 2006, 42.

22. Gerald L. Houseman, *Questioning the Law in Corporate America: An Agenda for Reform* (Westport, CT: Greenwood Press, 1993), Chapter 5.

23. Some of the financial publications claim that a popular film of 1987, *Wall Street*, helped to perpetuate this myth; see Andrew Serwer, "Let's Make a Deal," *Fortune*, June 13, 2005, 51–58.

24. David F. Swensen, *Unconventional Success: A Fundamental Approach to Personal Investment* (New York: Free Press, 2005).

25. Carl L. Reisner, "Roundtable: Key Legal Issues in Acquisitions and Defenses," *Mergers and Acquisitions* 20 (Summer, 1985), 32.

26. *Questioning the Law in Corporate America*, Chapters 3 and 4.

27. Stiglitz, "How to Fix the Global Economy," *New York Times*, October 3, 2006. In this op-ed piece, he states that this kind of fixing must "start with a responsible fiscal policy at home."

28. *Ibid.*

29. *Ibid.*

30. *Ibid.*

31. Stiglitz, *Making Globalization Work*, xii. On the following page he points out that the deepest flaw in International Monetary Fund (IMF) policies and procedures is found in that institution's "market fundamentalism," the belief that markets by themselves can lead to economic efficiency. See xiii, xiv–xv.

32. "The Economic Gauge That Can't Count," *This Week*, October 9, 2006, 42. Stiglitz admires the late iconoclastic economist E. F. Schumacher, who long ago argued that, as a matter of policy, fossil fuels should be extracted from the earth and used only in the most dire emergencies; see *Small Is Beautiful: Economics As If People Mattered: 25 Years Later, With Commentaries* (Point Roberts, Washington: Hartley and Marks, 1999).

33. Stiglitz and Bruce Greenwald, "Externalities in Economies With Imperfect Information and Incomplete Markets," *Quarterly Journal of Economics* 101 (May, 1986), 229–64.

34. There is nothing about information economics nor its Prize-winning scholars, for example, in N. Gregory Mankiw, *Macroeconomics* (fifth edition), (New York: Worth, 2003), one of the leading texts, but this is not at all a unique case. One of the leading texts in economic development, on the other hand, actually devotes nineteen pages of discussion to Stiglitz and his work; see E. Wayne Nafziger, *Economic Development* (fourth edition), (New York: Cambridge University Press, 2006). It has been reported that *Globalization and Its Discontents* receives its share of attention in grad-level courses devoted to International Political Economy; see Gregory W. White, "International Political Economy and the Persistent Scare Quotes Around 'Development,'" cited above.

35. *Economics for an Imperfect World.*

36. It should be explained that Australia has a saying, which many say is a longstanding tradition, of "cutting down the tall poppies." Social observers call this the "tall poppy syndrome." It refers to eliminating privilege and inequities within the

society in favor of a focus upon income equalization, strong trade unions, and Socialist values. Howard recently stated, "If there's one thing we need to get rid of in this country it is our tall poppy syndrome"; Philip Bowring column, *International Herald Tribune*, February 27, 2007.

37. "Leader of Britain's Conservatives Claims Political 'Center Ground,'" *New York Times*, October 2, 2006. This article discusses the Tories' explicit rejection of Thatcherism.

38. Stiglitz's particular and pointed disdain for Thatcher is found in the many references his books make to "Reagan-Thatcher" policies or approaches for developing nations; one of the many examples of this appears in *Globalization and Its Discontents*, 65.

39. Paul Kruger column, *International Herald Tribune*, December 26, 2006.

40. Orszag testimony to Congress, C-Span broadcast, January 28, 2007.

CHAPTER 4

1. *Globalization and Its Discontents*, Chapter 3. Former Federal Reserve Chair Alan Greenspan, who continues to offer commentary on the markets, uses the "invisible hand" term frequently.

2. The term "American aid" is used broadly here; some of it is sponsored by the IMF, World Bank, the UN, regional banks, and NGOs, but approval of the U. S. Government is often or usually an essential part of most aid decisions.

3. Steven Kinzer, *Overthrow: America's Century of Regime Change from Hawaii to Iraq* (New York: Times Books, 2006); Greg Grandin, *Empire's Workshop: Latin America, the United States, and the Rise of the New Imperialism* (New York: Metropolitan, 2006); Naomi Klein, *The Shock Doctrine: The Rise of Disaster Capitalism*.

4. *Globalization and Its Discontents*, 74–76.

5. Associated Press report, September 20, 2006.

6. Amy Chua, *World on Fire: How Exporting Free World Democracy Breeds Ethnic Hatred and Global Instability* (London: Heinemann, 2004).

7. Easterly, *The Elusive Quest for Growth: Economists' Adventures and Misadventures in the Tropics* (Cambridge: MIT Press, 2001).

8. Jagdish Bhagwati, *In Defense of Globalization* (New York: Oxford University Press, 2004); Martin Wolf, *Why Globalization Works* (New Haven: Yale University Press, 2004). Wolf's effort is data-heavy, but this does not carry his argument as far as he apparently thinks it does. A biting critique of the IMF, the World Bank, and the WTO is found in William Tabb, *Economic Governance in the Age of Globalization* (New York: Columbia University Press, 2004), which supports Stiglitz's view, by and large, while he crosses swords quite effectively with Bhagwati and Wolf.

9. Quoted by Jeff Faux of the Economic Policy Institute, January 11, 2007, at www.shared prosperity.org.

10. (New York: Oxford University Press, 2005).

11. (New York: Cambridge University Press, 2003).

12. A "go-go-free enterprise" approach is taken by Thomas L. Friedman in his best-selling *The World is Flat: A History of the Twenty-first Century* (New York: Farrar, Strauss, and Giroux, 2005). Stiglitz specifically rejects this hoopla and its assumptions that

the world economy is a level playing field in *Making Globalization Work*, 56. A different and more thoughtful but also myopic view of development can be seen in Jagdish Bhagwati, *Free Trade Today* (Princeton: Princeton University Press, 2002).

13. *Globalization and Its Discontents*, 9.

14. Quoted by Kamal Nath, India's Minister of Commerce and Industry, in Daniel Altman, "Managing Globalization," *International Herald Tribune*, February 28, 2007.

15. Steven Weber, Naazneen Barma, Matthew Kroenig, and Eli Ratner, "How Globalization Went Bad," *Foreign Policy* (January/February, 2007), 48–55.

16. Chalmers A. Johnson, *The Sorrows of Empire: Militarism, Secrecy, and the End of the Republic* (New York: Metropolitan, 2004).

17. *Ibid.*

18. Gerald L. Houseman, *Researching Indonesia: A Guide to Political Analysis.*

19. Interview of Stiglitz by Daniel Altman, *International Herald Tribune*, February 14, 2007; *Globalization and Its Discontents*, 3. The Seattle city government now concedes that 175 illegal arrests took place during these demonstrations.

20. Quoted by Greg Palast (staff writer, London *Observer*) website, October 10, 2001.

21. *Multinational Monitor* for July/August, 2006, for example, contains articles on the World Bank's promotion of deregulation schemes at the expense of workers, IMF promotion of union-busting in Indonesia and Mexico, and environmental dangers uncovered in Ghana.

22. Houseman, *Researching Indonesia.* The Iraq War has had a measurable effect upon opinions in countries like Indonesia, which has the largest Muslim population of any country in the world.

23. Greg Palast website, October 10, 2001.

24. Stiglitz has done three extensive treatises on globalization—*Globalization and Its Discontents* and *Making Globalization Work*, both cited above, and *Fair Trade for All: How Trade Can Promote Development*, coauthored with Andrew Charlton (New York: Oxford University Press, 2003). The latter can be described as the most technical approach to these issues, and it contains many useful charts and appendices. The strongest critiques of the World Bank and the International Monetary Fund appear in *Globalization and Its Discontents*, while many of the policy recommendations listed and discussed here are advocated and explained in *Making Globalization Work.*

25. "Economic Development with Unlimited Supplies of Labour," *Manchester School* 22 (1954), 139–91.

26. Gerald L. Houseman, *America and the Pacific Rim: Coming to Terms with New Realities* (Boulder: Rowman and Littlefield, 1995), Chapter 2.

27. *Globalization and Its Discontents*, 79.

28. James Surowiecki, "A Farewell to Alms?" *New Yorker* (July 25, 2005), 40.

29. Moseley, "The Demise of Development," *International Herald Tribune*, August 9, 2006.

30. Quoted by Palast website, October 10, 2001.

31. *Ibid.*

32. *Joseph Stiglitz and the World Bank: The Rebel Within*, Ha Joon Chang (ed.), (London: Anthem Press, 2001), 1–2.

33. Palast website, October 10, 2001.

34. *Ibid.* Stiglitz has presented lectures here and there emphasizing these very points; see *The Rebel Within.*

35. Quoted by Walden Bello, *Deglobalization: Ideas for a New World Economy* (London: Zed Books, 2004), 50.

36. *Ibid.*, 50.

37. Palast website, October 10, 2001. Sometimes other allocations of assets appear in this fourth phase; Stiglitz states in the Palast interview that the unsuccessful Russian bail-out of the early 1990's provided Boris Yeltsin with campaign money; this was considered a bonus because the IMF and the World Bank wanted him to win the election.

38. The late Professor Friedman, an earlier Nobel Prize winner for his work on consumer choice and on monetarism, was associated with the University of Chicago and later the Hoover Institution. The theme of "free enterprise" pervades his books and studies and was a consistent emphasis of his *Newsweek* column. He was an admirer of Hong Kong's free-wheeling and unregulated economy before it was annexed by China in 1997 and he was a major adviser and shameful apologist for the CIA-installed fascistic regime of the brutal General Augusto Pinochet in Chile. His influence, it must be admitted, spread itself far and wide. The so-called "Berkeley Mafia," the economic advisers clustered around the late genocidal monster and kleptocrat Suharto in Indonesia, were avid followers of the "Chicago school" despite their West Coast origins.

39. Palast interview.

40. *Making Globalization Work*, 176–84.

41. Robert Kuttner, "Trading Places," *International Herald Tribune*, December 27, 2006.

42. *Fair Trade for All*, 117.

43. *Making Globalization Work*, 228–31.

44. Sachs, *The End of Poverty: Economic Possibilities for Our Time* (New York: Penguin, 2005).

45. *Making Globalization Work*, 234–44.

46. This appears in an Oxfam International report set out at apporea.org (2006).

47. Oxfam report.

48. *Making Globalization Work*, 115–16.

49. *Ibid.*, 117.

50. *Ibid.*, 118.

51. Lila Rajiva, "Globalization Has Harmed Developing Nations," in *Globalization*, Louise I. Gerdes (ed.), (Chicago: Greenhaven Press, 2006), 126–40.

52. *Making Globalization Work*, 123–24. For an opposite (though certainly not apposite) treatment of the drug industry and the questions of innovation and regulation, see Richard A. Epstein, *Overdose: How Excessive Government Regulation Stifles Pharmaceutical Innovation* (New Haven: Yale University Press, 2006). This author does not take into account the heavily subsidized realities of the economics of the drug industry; he is apparently working in the train of the old-time medicine wagons and shows that once drew attention.

CHAPTER 5

1. Stiglitz, *The Roaring Twenties*, 21.

2. "Idle Contractors Add Millions to Iraq Rebuilding," *New York Times*, October 25, 2006.

3. This has not been for a lack of trying. In the late 1940s, destruction of many transit systems was carried out by the illegal and conspiratorial policies and actions of a General Motors subsidiary. The corporation entered a guilty plea in this anti-trust case. This is documented in a government publication known as the Snell Report; see Gerald L. Houseman, *The Right of Mobility* (Port Washington, NY: Kennikat, 1979).

4. *Ibid.*, 54–59; *The Roaring Nineties*, 53, 106–14, 193–98.

5. *Globalization and Its Discontents*, 54–59.

6. Daniel Altman, "Managing Globalization" (an interview of Stiglitz), *International Herald Tribune*, February 14, 2007.

7. Some of the literature available in this area that has proved helpful: *The Distributional Impact of Privatization in Developing Countries*, John Nellis and Nancy Birdsall (eds.), (Washington: Center for Global Development, 2005); Graeme A. Hodge, *Privatization: An International Review of Performance* (Boulder: Westview Press, 2000); *Limits to Privatization: How to Avoid Too Much of a Good Thing*, Ernst von Weizsacker, Oran Young, and Matthias Finger (eds.), (London: Earthscan, 2005); Hella Engerer, *Privatization and Its Limits in Central and Eastern Europe: Property Rights in Transition* (New York: Palgrave, 2001); Chrystia Freeland, *Sale of the Century: The Inside Story of the Second Russian Revolution* (New York: Crown, 2003); Jeffrey J. Leitzinger and Joseph E. Stiglitz, "Information Externalities in Oil and Gas Leasing," *Contemporary Economic Policy* 1 (undated), 44–57.

8. The book which includes more of his work on this subject than any other is *Whither Socialism?, op. cit.*

9. *Whither Socialism?*, 178–79.

10. *Ibid.*

11. "The Best Health Care in the U. S.," *Business Week*, July 17, 2006, 50–56 (on VA); *New York Times*, March 12, 2007 (on Walter Reed).

12. *Whither Socialism?*

13. *International Herald Tribune*, August 24, 2005.

14. Doug Orr, "Social Security Isn't Broken," *Dollars and Sense* (November/December, 2004), 14–22. Professor Orr, of Eastern Washington University, also provides an effective list of "Selective Readings on the Phony Crisis of Social Security and the Very Real Crisis in Private Pensions," a handout.

15. Bill Moyers, "A New Story for America," *Nation* (January 22, 2007), 12.

16. *Making Globalization Work*, 158–59.

17. *Multinational Monitor*, cited above, is a publication of Ralph Nader's Public Citizen organization, and it provides worthwhile information as well as a constant reminder of the shortcomings of corporations; its website is multinationalmonitor.org/monitor.html. Also pertinent for our purposes are two works of William E. Greider, *One World, Ready or Not: The Manic Logic of Global Capitalism* (New York: Simon and Schuster, 1997) and *The Soul of Capitalism: Opening Paths to a Moral Economy* (New York: Simon and Schuster, 2003) as well as David Korten, *When Corporations Rule the World* (second edition), (Bloomfield, CT: Kumarian, 2001) and Gerald L. Houseman, *Questioning the Law in Corporate America: An Agenda for Reform* (Westport, CT: Greenwood Press, 1993). It is well-recognized that several strongly-paced and successful economies in East Asia have achieved notice and some acclaim, beginning in the early 1980s, for pulling themselves out of poverty and achieving in-

novative niches in the international economy. South Korea, Taiwan, Malaysia and Singapore have been notable examples, and in each case the country can claim that this progress was achieved largely on its own. The key to their growth and the earlier success of Japan was simply based upon extraordinarily heavy inputs of capital and labor; see Paul Krugman, "The Myth of Asia's Miracle," *Foreign Affairs* 73 (November/December, 1994), 62–78.

18. *Globalization and Its Discontents*, 72–73.

19. *The Roaring Nineties*, 96–101.

20. *The Roaring Nineties*, 136–39.

21. *The Roaring Nineties*, 87–88. The absurd and totally ideological deregulation crusade of the Reagan Administration has been blamed by Stiglitz and others as the beginning of much of this hysteria; and this is well-documented in Martin and Susan Tolchin, *Selling Our Security: The Erosion of America's Assets* (New York: Knopf, 1992).

22. *Spokesman-Review* (Spokane), August 25, 2005.

23. Stiglitz and Greenwald, "Externalities in Economies with Incomplete Information and Incomplete Markets," *Quarterly Journal of Economics* 101 (May, 1986), 229–64.

24. Richard Parker, *John Kenneth Galbraith: His Life, His Politics, His Economics* (New York: Farrar, Strauss, and Giroux, 2005), 552–54.

25. John Kenneth Galbraith, *The Great Crash—1929* (New York: Houghton Mifflin, 1954).

CHAPTER 6

1. W. R. Scott, *The Constitution and Finance of English, Scottish, and Irish Joint Stock Companies to 1720* (Cambridge: Cambridge University Press, 1910–1912), ii, 37.

2. Joseph S. Davis, *Essays in the Earlier History of American Corporations* (two volumes), (Cambridge: Cambridge University Press, 1917), 4–5.

3. Sheryl J. Wragg, "Corporate Homicide: Will Michigan Follow Suit?" *University of Detroit Law Review* 62 (Fall, 1984), 67.

4. Ronald E. Seavoy, *The Origins of the American Business Corporation, 1784–1855* (Westport, CT: Greenwood Press, 1982), xii and Chapters 1 and 2.

5. 17 U. S. (4 Wheat. 518), 4 L.Ed. 629 (1819).

6. *Jones and Laughlin v. NLRB*, 301 U. S. 1, 81 L.Ed. 893 (1937).

7. "Participation and Development: Perspectives from the Comprehensive Development Paradigm," in *The Rebel Within: Joseph Stiglitz and the World Bank*, Ha-Joon Chang (ed.), (London: Anthem Press, 2001), 223–26.

8. "Proxy-Season Gridlock at the SEC," *Business Week*, February 19, 2007, 40.

9. John K. Galbraith, *The New Industrial State* (Boston: Houghton Mifflin, 1978).

10. These are the obvious and persistent themes of the three tomes Stiglitz devotes to the issues of globalization (see above); a good encapsulated summary of these concerns is found in an op-ed written by Stiglitz, "We Have Become Rich Countries of Poor People," *Financial Times* (London), September 8, 2006.

11. One asset is the support of the International Labor Organization (ILO), the UN agency that more than occasionally crosses swords with the WTO and employer groups.

12. Ted Nace, *Gangs of America: The Rise of Corporate Power and the Disabling of Democracy* (San Francisco: Barrett-Koehler, 2003).

13. Carole Pateman, *Participation and Democratic Theory* (New York: Cambridge University Press, 1970).

14. Barbara Ehrenreich, *Bait and Switch: The (Futile) Pursuit of the American Dream* (New York: Henry Holt, 2005); Ehrenreich, *Nickel and Dimed: On (Not) Getting By in America* (New York: Henry Holt, 2002).

15. Stiglitz, "Democratic Development as the Fruits of Labor," a speech which serves as Chapter 9 of *The Rebel Within*, Ha-Joon Chang (ed.), op. cit.

16. "The National Labor Relations Board Has Authority to Order an Employer to Bargain with a Labor Organization When the Employer Has Committed Egregious Unfair Labor Practices, Despite the Absence of a Union Count Majority or Election Victory," *University of Cincinnati Law Review* 50 (1981), 405–14.

Appendix A: Landmarks in the Evolution of the Economics of Information

1970 Questioning of the bargaining process and its outcomes is initiated by George Akerlof, "The Market for Lemons: Quality Uncertainty and the Market Mechanism," *Quarterly Journal of Economics* 84 (1970), 485–500, which took a new look at the perennial problem of purchasing a car.

1974 Joseph E. Stiglitz raises questions touching upon information issues in "Incentives and Risk-Sharing in Share-Cropping," *Review of Economic Studies* 41 (1974), 219–75; this also presages his interest in less-developed countries, where share-cropping is a common and normal arrangement in agriculture. A. Michael Spence introduces dynamics of market economies which point towards the eventual founding of information economics in *Market Signaling* (Cambridge: Harvard University Press, 1974).

Joseph E. Stiglitz embraces major arguments of the environmentalist movement as making good sense in economic terms in "Growth with Exhaustible Natural Resources: Efficient and Optimal Growth Paths," *Review of Economic Studies* 41 (1974), 123–38; this presages his support for environmental considerations in trade agreements, aid programs, and policies of organizations like the World Bank, IMF, and the WTO.

1977 Stiglitz publishes "Monopoly, Non-Linear Pricing, and Imperfect Information: The Insurance Market," *Review of Economic*

	Studies (1977), 407–30, an article which moves him firmly into the milieu of the economics of information.
1986	The world's full and clear introduction to the economics of information arrives with publication of a landmark article by Joseph E. Stiglitz and Bruce Greenwald, "Externalities in Economies with Imperfect Information and Incomplete Markets," *Quarterly Journal of Economics* 101 (May, 1986), 229–64.
1993–1997	Stiglitz serves on the Council of Economic Advisers in the Clinton Administration; he chairs the Council from 1995 to 1997.
1996	Publication of Stiglitz's *Whither Socialism?* by MIT Press.
1997–2000	Stiglitz serves as Chief Economist and Senior Vice-President of the World Bank, a position which, more than any other, serves as a catalyst for his work on issues of trade, aid, development, and the world's poor.
2001	Nobel Prize in Economics awarded to George Akerlof, Michael Spence, and Joseph E. Stiglitz for founding and researching the economics of information. Publication of *Joseph Stiglitz and the World Bank: The Rebel Within*, a collection of Stiglitz speeches edited, with a commentary, by Ha-Joon Chang, by Anthem Press.
2002	Publication of Stiglitz's *Globalization and Its Discontents* by W. W. Norton.
2003	Publication of Stiglitz's *The Roaring Nineties: A New History of the World's Most Prosperous Decade* by W. W. Norton. Publication of Stiglitz and Bruce Greenwald, *Towards a New Paradigm in Monetary Economics* by Cambridge University Press.
2003	Publication of the *festschrift* entitled *Economics for an Imperfect World: Essays in Honor of Joseph E. Stiglitz*, edited by Richard Arnott, Bruce Greenwald, Ravi Kanbur, and Barry Nalebuff, by MIT Press.
2005	Publication of a book by Stiglitz and Andrew Charlton, *Fair Trade for All: How Trade Can Promote Development* by Oxford University Press.
2006	Publication of Stiglitz's *Making Globalization Work* by W. W. Norton. The years since perhaps around 1994 have seen the rise of Stiglitz as a favorite speaker on the lecture circuit, as an interviewee in the electronic media and in newspapers, and as a frequent op-ed contributor to many publications.

Appendix B: Research Contributions of George Akerlof, Michael Spence, and Bruce C. N. Greenwald

George Akerlof and Michael Spence, two of the recipients of the Nobel Prize in Economics in 2001, have set standards of excellence in both their individual and joint contributions to research and economic thought, and it is obvious they have done more than their share to raise the levels of achievement within their discipline. Professor Bruce Greenwald of Columbia University, who has won many awards both for research and teaching, has co-authored a number of works with Joseph Stiglitz, including their book on monetary policy and their definitive article on the economics of information published in 1986.

GEORGE AKERLOF

Akerlof has been Professor of Economics at the University of California–Berkeley since 1980 and a Senior Fellow at the Brookings Institution since 1994. He was Cassel Professor (a position in which he specialized in money and banking) at the London School of Economics, 1978–1980, and Visiting Research Economist, Special Studies Section, Board of Governors of the Federal Reserve System from 1977 to 1978; and he has served, among other positions, as a Senior Staff Economist with the Council of Economic Advisers from 1973 to 1974.

He has served in any number of positions in academic associations and has been an editor of their journals, including the *American Economic Review* and the *Quarterly Journal of Economics.* He has also been the recipient of a long list of academic honors, though it is assumed that the Nobel ranks highest among these. His works are varied, but it is easily ascertained from his list of publications that he has taken a special interest in monetary policy, wage levels, and unemployment, and, of course, the economics of information. Perhaps one of the most interesting articles he has written is "The Case Against Conservative Macro Economics," which appeared in *Economica* in August, 1979. As this title indicates, Akerlof has a sharply political thrust in many of his works. In a 2003 address to *Der Spiegel* in Germany, according to many reports and blog sites, Akerlof told his audience, "This is the worst government the U. S. has ever had in its more than two hundred years of history . . . this is not normal government policy. What we have here is a form of looting."

The economics of information gained a greater footing as a result of Akerlof's 1970 article, cited in Appendix A, which showed how a failure in markets can arise when a seller of automobiles does not share honest and complete information about the quality of a car with buyers. Such asymmetry in information, he was able to show, will drive honest dealings out of such a market altogether unless this is overcome with new practices or, more likely, with new rules or regulations.

Regulations adopted to meet this need will of course be a burden for honest dealers because of the lack of scruples of what may well be a minority of dealers, but reasonable and sound laws are justified in this situation to make up for the failures of the market system.

Akerlof was born in 1940 in New Haven, Connecticut. His B. A. Degree is from Yale University in 1962, and his Ph.D. was awarded by MIT in 1966. His wife, Janet Yellen, is also an economist and an occasional co-collaborator.

MICHAEL SPENCE

Michael Spence is a Senior Fellow at the Hoover Institution and is the Philip H. Knight Professor Emeritus of Management in the Graduate School of Business at Stanford University. He served as Knight Professor from 1990 until 1999 and was also the Dean of the Stanford Business School during these years.

He held an appointment at Harvard from 1975 to 1990 as a Professor of Economics and Business Administration; in 1983 he was named chairman of the Economics Department and George Gund Professor of Economics and Business Administration. In 1978 Spence was awarded the John Kenneth Galbraith Prize for excellence in teaching, and he also received the John Bates Clark Medal in 1981 for a "significant contribution to economic thought and knowledge." This contribution was Spence's original work in job-market signaling, which proved to be one of the important keys to the development of the economics of information; he set up a model which has stimulated a great deal of new literature affecting this area of contract theory. The model illustrates that obtaining various well-regarded and expensive degrees provides a signal to employers, who have been shown to be willing to pay their employees for these qualifications. The implications of this model are manifestly connected to the economics of information. Spence's book on market signaling appeared in 1974 (cited in Appendix A). He is also the coauthor of several studies hailed as uniquely significant, including *Competition in the Investment Banking Industry* with Samuel L. Hayes and David Van Praag Marks (Cambridge: Harvard University Press, 1983); *Competition in the Open Economy: A Model Applied to Canada* with Richard E. Caves, Michael E. Potter, and John T. Scott (Harvard, 1980); and *International Competition*, which was coauthored with Heather A. Hazard (Cambridge: Ballinger, 1988).

Spence has also made a considerable mark in administration. In addition to the posts listed above, he was Dean of the Faculty of Arts and Sciences at Harvard from 1984 until 1990. He has received many honors, notably as a fellow of the American Academy of Arts and Sciences in 1983; the Nobel Prize caps off a brilliant career. Spence has also served on the editorial boards of four journals, including the *American Economic Review*. He was Chairman of the National Research Council Board on Science, Technology, and Economic Policy from 1991 to 1997.

His doctorate is from Harvard University (1972) and he has two B. A. degrees—one from Princeton and one from Oxford. The latter degree was achieved because he was named a Rhodes Scholar after receiving his degree in Mathematics at Princeton in 1966. Spence was born in 1943 in Montclair, New Jersey, and spent a good part of his early years in Canada.

BRUCE C. N. GREENWALD

Bruce C. N. Greenwald is the Robert Heilbrunn Professor of Finance and Asset Management in the Columbia Business School, where he is Director of the Heilbrunn Center for Graham and Dodd Investing. In addition to his groundbreaking work on the economics of information, he is considered a Wall Street guru on value investments; and he is a recognized expert on productivity and the globalization of markets.

Greenwald, whose earlier degrees are in Electrical Engineering, received his Ph.D. in Economics from MIT in 1978. His earlier appointments include stints at the Bureau of the Budget and Wesleyan, Harvard, and Princeton universities. He is a popular teacher whose courses are invariably oversubscribed, and he has been honored with the Columbia Presidential Teaching Award. His books include *Value Investing: From Graham to Buffett and Beyond*, a work of great practical merit published by John Wiley in 2001, and *Towards a New Paradigm of Monetary Economics*, coauthored with Stiglitz and published by Cambridge University Press in 2003. He is also Stiglitz's coauthor of the landmark article, "Externalities in Economics with Imperfect Information and Incomplete Markets," which appears in the *Quarterly Journal of Economics* (May, 1986).

He has coauthored eighteen articles with Stiglitz, many or most of them dealing with one or another aspect of the economics of information. Greenwald's website provides a complete listing, but noteworthy examples are "Labor Market Adjustments and the Persistence of Unemployment," *American Economic Review*, May, 1995; "Information, Finance, and Markets: The Architecture of Allocative Mechanisms," *Journal of Industrial and Corporate Change*, November, 1992; "Macro-economic Models of Equity and Credit Rationing," a chapter in *Asymmetric Information, Corporate Finance, and Investment*, R. G. Hubbard (ed.), (Chicago: University of Chicago Press, 1990); "Asymmetric Information and the New Theory of the Firm: Financial Constraints and Risk Behavior," *American Economic Review*, May, 1990; and "Pareto Inefficiencies of Market Economies: Search and Efficiency Wage Models," *American Economic Review*, May, 1998.

Much of Greenwald's work with Stiglitz, as well as the work he has produced on his own, contributed at least indirectly to his coauthor's Nobel Prize triumph; this appears to be appreciated by any number of observers.

Appendix C: Organizations Now Without Purpose as a Result of the Findings of the Economics of Information

> . . . contrary to what we have heard for a generation now, the individualist, greed-driven, free-market ideology is at odds with our history and with what most Americans really care about . . . more people agree that inequality is bad, . . . that corporations have too much power, that money . . . is corrupting democracy and that working families and [the] poor need and deserve help when the market system fails. . . . Indeed, the American public is committed to a set of values that almost perfectly contradicts the conservative agenda that has dominated politics for a generation now.
>
> —Bill Moyers, "A New Story for America," *Nation*, January 22, 2007, p. 12

The Nobel Prize winners of 2001 have proved that "free enterprise" does not exist. Not even the mystical "invisible hand" envisioned by Adam Smith can be rationally claimed to be a market factor. More than twenty years have passed since the economics of information came into being, proving this and other valid points about market economies.

A vast number of writers, both academic and journalistic, have all the same failed to pick up on this point. There can be no absolute certainty why this is the case. It could certainly be and probably is, in the worst instances, a willful neglect rooted in some pathetic ideological need.

There are obvious kinds of rationalization at work. A handful of scholars bent on the "free enterprise" cause, for example, have continued their work while supposedly incorporating the economics of information into their considerations. This is the case, however, only in the names, mottoes, or titles of institutes or their manifestoes. Their actual work goes on the same as before, as though the work of Akerlof, Spence, Stiglitz, Greenwald and others did not exist. This is primarily an ideological tack in motive and tone, and neither their conclusions nor their "methodology" take any of this work into account. Mediocre to the core of their being, they continue to discuss "free enterprise" and other representative terms while acknowledging the changed universe, in the offhand manner of a phrase or a barely-noticeable footnote, which amounts of course to a gross contradiction. Those who acknowledge the economics of information in this way are not much better in their analyses, as one would expect, than the vast majority of "free enterprisers" who do not mention it at all.

The far more likely situation found in this vast wilderness, however, is a failure to even acknowledge this decades-old phenomenon. It has to be concluded that this is often done with a willful motive or because of a severe and unwarranted ignorance of the domain of findings relevant to the disciplines of economics or political economy. A lack of such willfulness is to be hoped for, but it has to be admitted and realized that picking out relative virtues in such a swamp is neither worth our time nor within any reasonable range of our capabilities. It is assumed here, all the same, that many writers, orators, electronic media people, propagandists, and (sad to say) economists and political scientists are guilty of this omission because of an inexcusable lack; they are, quite obviously, ill-informed.

Such neglect in the case of organizations is doubly damning; for someone in the office or found in the ranks should be, at the very least, ever so faintly aware of what is occurring in the world, especially if it involves a matter that falls within some realm of their undertakings. A list of organizations that have failed to get the point is offered here because the public can assuredly benefit from knowing that while some organizations are on top of the changes going on Out There, many prominent ones are not. This is necessarily a partial listing, since the number of political and economic groups goes into the tens of thousands (if not the hundreds of thousands, in the internet age), but a strong effort has been made to identify the most important among these.

The omission of the economics of information and, instead, an insistent use of the now-shunned (by science) "free enterprise" term is characteristic of all of the groups listed below. This should be embarrassing, to be sure, but it also raises questions about the goals and purposes of such organizations. In some cases, these are conservative organizations who support "free enterprise" but also have concerns in other issue areas that one could argue—though not very cogently—are not connected with economics. One might suppose that they could find a renewed purpose by somehow jettisoning economic issues and staying with their other claims based upon moral precepts, or public needs, or other criteria. In many or most cases, however, these are conservative organizations who have decided, at one time or another, to put "free enterprise" issues into front and center positions. These organizations may not know about the intellectual crisis they have brought upon themselves through their neglect, willful or otherwise. A re-do of some kind is obviously in order unless they choose to continue looking ridiculous. But these quandaries are their business, not ours; I must admit that I have no great concern about the nature, reformation, or preservation of conservative organizations, though their so-called "think tanks" raise some important tax and policy questions (see below); their internal issues will therefore be left for them to sort out.

ORGANIZATIONS WHOSE LITERATURE AND/OR WEBSITES INDICATE CONTINUED FEALTY TO THE VIRTUES OF THE CAUSE OF "FREE ENTERPRISE" EVEN THOUGH IT DOES NOT EXIST

Adam Smith Institute, London (once supported a "head tax" Smith would have scorned)
American Conservative Union
American Enterprise Institute
American Family Association (boycotts!)
American Legislative Exchange Council
Americans for Tax Reform
Atlas Economic Research Foundation (sets up conservative think tanks)
Ayn Rand Institute
Bluegrass Institute for Public Policy Solutions
Bradley Foundation
Business and Industry Political Action Committee (BIPAC)
Campaign for Working Families Political Action Group
Cascade Policy Institute, Oregon (says we should "replace all state taxes with user fees")
Cato Institute (perhaps the foremost champion of "free enterprise")
Christian Coalition of America
Club for Growth
Collegiate Network (Adam Smithian)
Competitive Enterprise Institute
Concerned Women for America
Eagle Forum
Evergreen Research Foundation (narrow the electorate through enhanced "qualifications"!)
Family Research Council
Federalist Society for Law and Policy Studies
Foundation for Economic Education (one of the oldest of these organizations)

Free Congress Foundation
Free Enterprise Institute
Freedom Works
Heritage Foundation: possibly the largest
Hoover Institution
Hudson Institute
Independence Institute, Colorado
Independent Women's Forum
Institute for Justice
Institute for Policy Innovation
Institute of Economic Affairs, London (international in scope)
Intercollegiate Studies Institute
International Society for Individual Liberty (and state branches)
Leadership Institute (sells Adam Smith ties!)
Mackinac Center for Public Policy
Madison Project
Manhattan Institute
Mont Pelerin Society (F. Hayek's group)
National Center for Policy Analysis
National Right to Work Legal Foundation (antilabor union specialization)
Pioneer Institute for Public Policy Research
South Carolina Policy Council
State Policy Network (collection of state-level conservative think tanks)
Sutherland Institute, Utah
Texas Public Policy Foundation
Washington Legal Foundation
Young America's Foundation (sells Ann Coulter posters!)

THE TAX ISSUE RAISED BY CONSERVATIVE "THINK TANKS"

Conservative "think tanks" have enjoyed a growth pattern that is astonishing. Not very long ago these organizations were overwhelmingly situated, with a few notable exceptions, in Washington, D. C., and their focus was upon federal-level (or even broader) issues. Now, as the above list indicates, they are found at the state level as well, and their presence is notable, and indeed ubiquitous, in practically every state. This growth, it should be understood, does not arise from any noteworthy or even discernible public demand. It arises from a combination of right-wing ideologists and the tax code.

Wealthy oldsters or their scions decide that the temptation is too strong to resist: gifts of tax-sheltered money are provided so that these groups can set up research centers, sometimes with poshy surroundings and appointments, in which their scholars can work. The term "scholar" is probably a misnomer here, unless we limit its application to the efforts made; these could be carried out with an earnest level of scholarship in mind and—who are we to say?—with lofty goals of uncovering good-sized nuggets of truth from some basic or applied research. Giving conservative organizations the benefit of any of our doubts, however, would probably be a mistake.

We *can* judge the results, of course. I recall, for example, a study of pornography undertaken by one of the bigger conservative foundations in which they concluded, after a very short flurry of study and in a very brief publication, that yes, indeed, pornography was a direct and immediate cause of all sorts of pathologies and social problems. And this may well be the case; but I would argue that a seat-of-the-pants set of statements derived after just a few days of pondering the subject may not be a reliable source for approaching any definitive conclusions on this or any other subject. One of the more enthusiastic (and, frankly, quite entrepreneurial) state-level "think tank" leaders indicates that he can get a "study" out in a very short time, perhaps in only three days! (*New York Times*, November 16, 2006). No deep pondering is called for, and it should be conceded that this indeed would be a rare phenomenon in such an environment. Most pertinent to the concerns guiding the present study and the economics of information are the frequent, indeed constant, chirping of the directors of these "policy" groups about economic issues: they must take precedence over any other concerns of their organizations, their leaders and founders say, and the most pressing among these concerns is that of standing four-square behind the "free enterprise" system (*New York Times*, November 16, 2006) even though twenty years and five months had passed at this time since publication of the landmark article on the economics of information. Since they insist that this is the case, it is manifestly obvious that the first consideration they should take up is whether they should go out of business altogether, since the issue of "free enterprise" has been fully settled for a couple of decades.

What they are selling to the public, then, is a dethroned platitude and such accouterments as flat-rate tax systems, voucher systems for our schools, labor union-bashing, and one kind or another of the "incentives" so dear to Rightist prattlers who oppose social welfare programs for the poor while favoring tax and subsidy giveaways to corporations and the wealthy.

They have the right to do this, certainly; a democratic society must try to provide a forum for all sides of any question, and those sides must include the flat-earthers, the pre-Copernicans, and certainly the dinosaurs of the world of economics; and along with this right goes the freedom to exercise it, employing any legal or constitutional means deemed suitable or necessary, even in luxurious offices in Washington, New York, California, or Indianapolis.

But not at my expense! And not at yours, either! There is no good reason for supporting these faux research efforts with our tax money. Promote conservatism or "free enterprise" or a belief that the black holes in deep space are centered upon fried doughnuts if you like, but do not extract an involuntary toll from me for these reams and mountains of twaddle. It is not fair, and there has to be a legislative remedy for it. The remedy is simple enough: tax these one-sided foundations. That's right: tax them! If it is possible to ascertain from some on-high viewing platform that a foundation is really interested in scholarship rather than propaganda, a tax concession may be possible if some reasonable test is used. Barring this, any foundation that produces one right-wing tract after another for the cause of "free enterprise" and its policy offshoots should not be able to give a tax break to itself or any of its benefactors. Political organizations do not get tax breaks; political foundations should not, either.

Someone out there might agree that all of this is fine and dandy but will ask about the few (and usually not so well-off) foundations that tend to show a bias in favor of economic equality or labor rights or much-needed and steeply progressive taxation systems. What do we do about these liberal or leftish think tanks? The answer, obviously, is that they should be taxed as well.

How would all of this work out? It would be good for the revenue side of the government, of course, but more importantly it would be a recognition that, just as we should not have to pay for another person's prayer hut or church or mosque or synagogue, we should not have to pay for any of the propaganda produced by the "free enterprise" cultists nor by any other political ax-grinder. It would all be very neat, if you think about it, and it will certainly strike a blow for honesty and against hypocrisy.

Appendix D: The Altered Literature of Economics Within the Changed Universe

The economics of information and its corollary, the death of "free enterprise," requires a new or second look, for most of us, at some of the better-known though now thoroughly discredited works we have encountered through the years. Adam Smith, needless to say, remains an important historical figure in economics, even though most of his theoretical contributions, which he saw as moral guides and imperatives, have now been placed within their appropriate historical context. The seemingly endless production of books from the political Right, however, most or all of which pledge fealty to "free enterprise," whatever that is, may still have some very limited place in our consciousness as curiosities or novelties of some sort. Many of us, alas, have less shelf space than we would like, so this could mean that a great batch of writers, from Ayn Rand to Ludwig Von Mises or perhaps William F. Buckley, Jr., might have to be filed appropriately.

The changes wrought by the economics of information will affect this variety of efforts in various ways. The memoirs of Prime Minister Margaret Thatcher, for example, may be even less interesting than they were before. The books from the "law and economics" school at the University of Chicago, which never made much of an impact upon the popular realm, anyway, are now more dispensable than ever. It was always a difficult task, I am disposed to think, to impose micro or macro models over the reasoning processes developed through the hundreds of years of the evolution of law.

It is a good idea, all the same, to sift through this wreckage and examine, in some detail, what has happened to the so-called "classics" of "free enterprise." Space and time are necessarily limited here, although someone of historical bent might wish to go through the usual lists of such works in order to chart the casualties and damage. They would be required, unfortunately, to pay the cost of many hours lost in tedious reading, and I, for one, shall forego any such ambitious exercise because there are many more interesting tasks still in need of being done. But the ravaging effects of the economics of information and the death of "free enterprise" must be at least momentarily assessed in terms of its effects upon the literature of the discipline of political economy in order for us to appreciate just how much and how far the changed universe of economics now affects us and even enhances our lives.

So looking at one book can enable us, to some extent, to understand what has happened to this domain—this forest—by looking at one of its trees. Perhaps the most appropriate choice for this exercise, because of its presumed eminence and once-acclaimed scholarship, is F. A. Hayek's *The Road to Serfdom*, published by the University of Chicago Press in 1944.

If any work can be considered the "holy of holies" to those who cherish "free enterprise," Hayek is it. Hosannahs and paeans for him have appeared through the years in books, articles, journals, and even the more trashy magazines of the Right and, on markedly fewer occasions, in other publications as well. The historical significance of Hayek may have developed, more than by any factor, in his provision of a base for argumentation—perhaps we should call it a "home"—for the distraught conservatives trying to bear up during the time of overwhelming influence, honors, acceptance, and (most certainly) ascendancy of the work of John Maynard Keynes in the years following the Great Depression. Hayek resented the great approval accorded Keynesian economics and sought to challenge and answer it. He had been a Socialist briefly before finding his true path, which we are to take to mean a road to freedom founded upon a libertarian approach guided by personal choices, property rights, and market forces.

His most profound objections are grounded upon state intervention into economic and personal life. He drew heavily upon the experiences of Europe in the 1930s and 1940s, when Hitler and Stalin proved that state prerogatives could very well lead to human suffering as well as societal breakdown and disaster. There can be no doubt that Hayek's abhorrence of super-states causing this massive amount of human misery is understandable and laudable, perhaps heroic. Against these evils he posited a "free enterprise system" respecting human dignity and freedom, including property rights, guided by noncoercive but efficient free market forces.

His problem with Keynes and supporters of the welfare state was founded upon the belief that *any* planning for growth in government programs or in enlarged responsibility to look after the economic needs of people was doomed to result, sooner or eventually, in statism quite along the lines set out by the Hitlerian or Stalinist models. Any compromise with the welfare state is therefore *verboten*. Oddly, and in spite of this, the language of this text seems to concede some need for limited measures aimed at the general good, though planning is described as the major freedom-destroying culprit. There is always a certain admiration most any of us can feel for a writer who proceeds from noncoercive premises, but Hayek's work is challenged, and indeed vitiated, by two insuperable problems. The first and most obvious one is that markets cannot be considered noncoercive, the point that Stiglitz and his associates have so stridently and successfully made. Asymmetries of information militate against Hayek and any outmoded "free enterprise" concept.

There is, as well, the devastating problem which appears when Hayek's work is arrayed against the evolution of the United States and Western Europe since the time of this writing. Coercive and antilibertarian forces of the political Right, assuredly evident in the Reagan and Thatcher years but achieving a new and wrenching dominance in the George W. Bush Administration, have removed any scary feelings we might have had about unemployment compensation, Medicare, or programs aimed at providing for nutritional needs of children. We must worry instead about electronic eavesdropping, preemptive wars of choice, the destruction of habeas corpus protections we have known since 1215, torture, Stalinist-styled extraordinary rendition, attacks upon the separation of powers through devices like signing statements attached to legislation, and an expanded role for the military-industrial complex, complete with the privatization, waste, and fraud revealed within the structures of our military adventures, and, not the least important consideration, the blessings of all of this that have come from conservative politicians, officials, magazines, web sites, and publicity flaks. As for the welfare state, it is increasingly threatened by the attacks launched against Social Security, veterans' benefits, Medicare and Medicaid, pensions, and freely-organized labor unions. The gross and threatening statism of this Neo-Conservative Age does not proceed from the welfare state or its activities or from its premises. It comes from the political forces that, as recently as in Reagan's time, postured about the need for smaller government, balanced budgets, and individual freedom. The most charitable remark we can make about Hayek is that he has missed the point entirely. *The Road to Serfdom*, it has turned out, was an anachronism by the time it first went into print.

Sadly, Hayek abandoned his fealty to libertarianism in the company of Thatcher and with the trips he made to the fascistic state headed by Chile's General Pinochet in the 1970s. He urged authoritarian measures upon both of these leaders, and he praised the murderous General by engaging in silly talk about the priorities of economic freedom over political freedom. This did a great deal, according to Naomi Klein and other reporters and observers, to discredit his earlier concerns. All of his work had been questionable, to say the least, but his admiration for this cruel dictator ripped away any credibility he may have developed over the years.

Bibliography

Arnott, Richard and Bruce Greenwald, Ravi Kanbur, and Barry Nalebuff (eds.) *Economics for an Imperfect World: Essays in Honor of Joseph E. Stiglitz*. Cambridge, MA: MIT Press, 2003. (Includes Nobel Prize speech.)

Boettke, Peter J. "Where Did Economics Go Wrong? Modern Economics as a Flight from Reality," *Critical Review* 11 (Winter, 1997), 11–64.

Bello, Waldo. *Deglobalization: Ideas for a New World Economy*. London: Zed, 2002.

———. *Dilemmas of Domination: The Unmaking of the American Empire*. New York: Henry Holt, 2005.

Chang, Ha-Joon. *Bad Samaritans: Trade and the Secret History of Capitalism*. London: Bloomsbury Press, 2008.

———. *Kicking Away the Ladder: Development Strategy in Historical Perspective*. London: Wimbledon, 2002.

———. (ed.) *The Rebel Within: Joseph Stiglitz and the World Bank*. London: Anthem Press, 2001.

Chang, Ha-Joon and Irene Grabel. *Reclaiming Development: An Alternative Economic Policy Manual*. London: Zed, 2005.

Cline, William R. *The United States as a Debtor Nation*. Washington, DC: Institute for International Economics, 2005.

Destler, I. M. *American Trade Politics* (fourth edition). Washington, D.C.: Institute for International Economics, 2005.

Dicken, Peter. *Global Shift: Mapping the Contours of the World Economy* (fifth edition.) New York: Guilford, 2007.

Faux, Jeff. *The Global Class War*. Hoboken, NJ: John Wiley, 2006.

Freeland, Chrystia. *Sale of the Century: The Inside Story of the Second Russian Revolution*. New York: Crown, 2003.

Galbraith, John Kenneth. *The New Industrial State*. Boston: Houghton Mifflin, 1978.

Grandin, Greg. *Empire's Workshop: Latin America, the United States, and the Rise of the New Imperialism*. New York: Henry Holt, 2006.

Greider, William. *One World, Ready or Not.* New York: Simon and Schuster, 1997.

Houseman, Gerald L. *America and the Pacific Rim: Coming to Terms with New Realities.* Boulder: Rowman and Littlefield, 1995.

——. *Questioning the Law in Corporate America: An Agenda for Reform.* Westport, CT: Greenwood Press, 1993.

——. *Researching Indonesia: A Guide to Political Analysis.* Lewiston, NY: Edwin Mellen Press, 2004.

International Monetary Fund. *World Economic Outlook: Financial Systems and Economic Cycles.* Washington, DC: IMF, 2006. (An annual report.)

Klein, Naomi. *The Shock Doctrine: The Rise of Disaster Capitalism.* New York: Metropolitan, 2007.

Kuttner, Robert. *Everything for Sale: The Virtues and Limits of Markets.* New York: Knopf, 1998.

Lind, Michael. *Up From Conservatism: Why the Right is Wrong for America.* New York: Free Press, 1996.

"Markets with Asymmetric Information." (a statement of the Nobel Prize Committee), October 10, 2001: www.nobelprize.org/economics/laureates/2001/ecoadv.pdf

Nafziger, E. Wayne. *Economic Development* (fourth edition). New York: Cambridge University Press, 2006.

Pateman, Carole. *Participation and Democratic Theory.* New York: Cambridge University Press, 1970.

Perelman, Michael. *Railroading Economics: The Creation of the Free Market Mythology.* New York: Monthly Review Press, 2006.

Perkins, John. *Confessions of an Economic Hit Man.* New York: Penguin, 2004.

Rotering, Frank M. *Needs and Limits: A New Economics for Sustainable Well-Being.* Brattleboro, VT: Rotering, 2007.

Sachs, Jeffrey. *The End of Poverty: Economic Possibilities for Our Time.* New York: Penguin, 2005.

Schumacher, E. F. *Small Is Beautiful: Economics As If People Mattered.* New York: Harper and Row, 1973.

Sen, Amartya. *On Ethics and Economics.* Oxford: Blackwell, 1978.

Shiva, Vandana and Radha Holla Bahr, and Afsar H. Jafri. *Corporate Highjack of Biodiversity: How WTO-TRIPS Rules Promote Corporate Hijack of Peoples' Biodiversity and Knowledge.* New Delhi: Navdanya, 2002.

Stiglitz, Joseph E. *Economics of the Public Sector* (third edition). New York: W. W. Norton, 2000.

——. *Globalization and Its Discontents.* New York: W. W. Norton, 2002.

——. *Making Globalization Work.* New York: W. W. Norton, 2006.

——. *The Roaring Nineties: A New History of the World's Most Prosperous Decade.* New York: W. W. Norton, 2003.

——. *Whither Socialism?* Cambridge, MA: MIT Press, 1996.

Stiglitz, Joseph E. and Andrew Charlton. *Fair Trade for All: How Trade Can Promote Development.* New York: Oxford University Press, 2005.

Stiglitz, Joseph E. and Bruce Greenwald, "Externalities in Economies with Incomplete Information and Incomplete Markets," *Quarterly Journal of Economics* 101 (May, 1986), 229–64.

——. *Towards a New Paradigm in Monetary Economics*. New York: Cambridge University Press, 2003.

Joseph E. Stiglitz and Linda J. Bilmes. *The Three-Trillion Dollar War: The True Cost of the Iraq Conflict*. New York: W. W. Norton, 2008.

Waligorski, Conrad P. *The Political Theory of Conservative Economists*. Lawrence, KS: University Press of Kansas, 1990.

Index

About the Author

Gerald L. Houseman is Professor Emeritus of Political Science, Indiana University-Fort Wayne, and he has most recently been associated with the graduate program in political science at Washington State University. His areas of study include political economy and economic development, Asian studies, trade issues, and social science methodology. He is the author of numerous articles and ten books, including *Researching Indonesia*, 2004; *America and the Pacific Rim: Coming to Terms with New Realities*, 1995; *Questioning the Law in Corporate America: An Agenda for Reform*, 1993; *Judging the Constitution* with co-editor Michael McCann, 1989; *City of the Right: Urban Applications of American Conservative Thought*, 1982; and, *The Right of Mobility*, 1979. He has served as a guest lecturer in Malaysia, Indonesia, and England, and has also carried out lectures and research in Pakistan, Thailand, Germany, Ireland, and Canada. He received the Wildavsky Award for Best Public Policy Article of the Year from the Policy Studies Organization in 1994; several Fulbright, NSF, APSA, and NEH awards; and many other awards, honors, and grants, and he is an associate member of the United Steelworkers of America, AFL-CIO.